MARK

FOLLOW ME

JAMES HOOVER

20 STUDIES
FOR INDIVIDUALS
OR GROUPS

ivp

Life
Builder
Study

INTER-VARSITY PRESS
36 Causton Street, London SW1P 4ST, England
Email: ivp@ivpbooks.com
Website: www.ivpbooks.com

Originally published in the United States of America in the LifeGuide® Bible Studies series in 1999 by InterVarsity Press, Downers Grove, Illinois
First published in Great Britain by Scripture Union in 2000
This edition published in Great Britain by Inter-Varsity Press 2019

British Library Cataloguing-in-Publication Data
A catalogue record for this book is available from the British Library.

ISBN: 978–1–78359–822–9

Printed in Great Britain by 4edge Limited

Inter-Varsity Press publishes Christian books that are true to the Bible and that communicate the gospel, develop discipleship and strengthen the church for its mission in the world.

IVP originated within the Inter-Varsity Fellowship, now the Universities and Colleges Christian Fellowship, a student movement connecting Christian Unions in universities and colleges throughout Great Britain, and a member movement of the International Fellowship of Evangelical Students. Website: www.uccf.org.uk. That historic association is maintained, and all senior IVP staff and committee members subscribe to the UCCF Basis of Faith.

Contents

Getting the Most Out of *Mark*

Few Westerners put much stock in royalty. The lives of the British royals have become a source of gossip rather than respect. We have been raised to treasure the spirit of democracy. But democracy, at least on any large scale, is a recent development in human history.

People in other eras were accustomed to kings. For good or evil, kings and emperors left their mark on daily life. Thus when a new king came to power, whether through natural succession or through defeat in battle, questions clamored in people's minds. What would the new king be like? Would he be kind and compassionate, or selfish and ruthless? Would he use his power to serve his own ends, or would he seek the welfare of all his subjects?

The Jews of Jesus' day, long oppressed by foreign rulers, yearned for a new king—one whom God himself would anoint and use to establish his own rule of justice and peace not only over Israel but over all the earth. Imagine the excitement then when John the Baptist came announcing the coming of the Lord as king and when Jesus himself announced, "The time has come. The kingdom of God is near." Yet as Jesus continued his ministry, he met a growing wave of opposition. Not everyone was pleased with the kind of kingdom he announced or with who he proclaimed himself to be. The religious rulers especially opposed him, but the common people heard him gladly.

Just the Facts

New Testament scholars, with few exceptions, agree that Mark's Gospel is the earliest written account of Jesus' life and ministry. Composed between A.D. 60 and 70, it likely served as the literary basis for the Gospels of Matthew and Luke. Mark himself, though not one of the Twelve, was probably an early convert (Acts 12:12) and a companion of both Peter (1 Peter 5:13) and Paul. Though Mark had an early falling out with Paul (Acts 15:36–41), the two were clearly reconciled later on (Colossians 4:10; 2 Timothy 4:11; Philemon 24). Thus Mark is linked to two of the most prominent apostles.

The broad consensus among scholars today is that Mark was not just a collector of stories about Jesus but that he molded and shaped these stories to create the literary form we recognize as a Gospel. Here in written form we find the first account of how God's promises in Isaiah to establish his rule are coming to pass through the life and teachings of Jesus the Messiah.

Pastoral concerns seem uppermost in Mark's mind. Ralph Martin and others have argued that Mark wrote to counteract some dangerous distortions of the gospel message.* Apparently some Christians so focused on Jesus' deity and glorious resurrection that they began to ignore his humanity and suffering. As a result they expected to be spared suffering in this life and to quickly join Jesus in the glories of heaven. You can well imagine how their faith was shaken when Nero took to using some of them as torches!

Mark, theologically and pastorally, sets out to retell the story of Jesus, showing that the kingdom in its glory comes at the end of the path of suffering and service. While Matthew focuses on Jesus as the teacher from whom we should learn (Matthew 11:29; 28:20) and John focuses on him as the Son of God in whom we should believe (John 20:31), Mark portrays Jesus principally as the servant-king whom we should follow (Mark 1:17). Thus, if we are to enjoy the glories of the kingdom, we too must follow the road of suffering and service.

This guide offers you the opportunity to learn through the eyes of Mark more about Jesus and the life he calls each of us to. It consists of twenty forty-five-minute studies, with the option of two review studies (one following study nine and the other following study twenty) that tie together major themes. The studies have been divided into two parts, nine in the first and eleven in the second, so that the whole Gospel can easily be studied in two quarters. Although these studies have been designed with believers in mind, they have been used successfully, with minor changes, in a mixed group of believers and inquirers into the faith.

May the Lord himself increase your understanding of who he is and the life to which he has called you.

---

*See Ralph Martin, *Mark: Evangelist and Theologian* (Zondervan, 1973). See also, R. A. Guelich, "Mark, Gospel of," in *Dictionary of Jesus and the Gospels*, ed. Joel B. Green, Scot McKnight and I. Howard Marshall (InterVarsity Press, 1992), pp. 512–25.

Suggestions for Individual Study

1. As you begin each study, pray that God will speak to you through his Word.

2. Read the introduction to the study and respond to the "personal reflection" question or exercise. This is designed to help you focus on God and on the theme of the study.

3. Each study deals with a particular passage, so that you can delve into the author's meaning in that context. Read and reread the passage to be studied. If you are studying a book, it will be helpful to read through the entire book prior to the first study. The questions are written using the language of the New International Version, so you may wish to use that version of the Bible. The New Revised Standard Version is also recommended.

4. This is an inductive Bible study, designed to help you discover for yourself what Scripture is saying. The study includes three types of questions. *Observation* questions ask about the basic facts: who, what, when, where and how. *Interpretation* questions delve into the meaning of the passage. *Application* questions help you discover the implications of the text for growing in Christ. These three keys unlock the treasures of Scripture.

5. Write your answers to the questions in the spaces provided or in a personal journal. Writing can bring clarity and deeper understanding of yourself and of God's Word.

6. It might be good to have a Bible dictionary handy. Use it to look up any unfamiliar words, names or places.

7. Use the prayer suggestion to guide you in thanking God for what you have learned and to pray about the applications that have come to mind.

8. You may want to go on to the suggestion under "Now or Later," or you may want to use that idea for your next study.

Suggestions for Members of a Group Study

1. Come to the study prepared. Follow the suggestions for individual

study mentioned above. You will find that careful preparation will greatly enrich your time spent in group discussion.

2. Be willing to participate in the discussion. The leader of your group will not be lecturing. Instead, he or she will be encouraging the members of the group to discuss what they have learned. The leader will be asking the questions that are found in this guide.

3. Stick to the topic being discussed. Your answers should be based on the verses that are the focus of the discussion and not on outside authorities such as commentaries or speakers. These studies focus on a particular passage of Scripture. Only rarely should you refer to other portions of the Bible. This allows for everyone to participate in in-depth study on equal ground.

4. Be sensitive to the other members of the group. Listen attentively when they describe what they have learned. You may be surprised by their insights! Each question assumes a variety of answers. Many questions do not have "right" answers, particularly questions that aim at meaning or application. Instead the questions push us to explore the passage more thoroughly

When possible, link what you say to the comments of others. Also be affirming whenever you can. This will encourage some of the more hesitant members of the group to participate.

5. Be careful not to dominate the discussion. We are sometimes so eager to express our thoughts that we leave little opportunity for others to respond. By all means participate! But allow others to do so too.

6. Expect God to teach you through the passage being discussed and through the other members of the group. Pray that you will have an enjoyable and profitable time together, but also that as a result of the study, you will find ways that you can take action individually and/or as a group.

7. Remember that anything said in the group is considered confidential and should not be discussed outside the group unless specific permission is given to do so.

8. If you are the group leader, you will find additional suggestions at the back of the guide.

1

Gospel Roots

Mark 1:1–13

Getting to know our family roots helps us to better understand who we are, and sharing family stories is often a great way to get to know other people.

GROUP DISCUSSION. Think of a story, picture or object in your family that links you to past generations. Explain to the group what this link to history means to you.

PERSONAL REFLECTION. Think of important people, events and places in your spiritual development. How have they shaped you? Give thanks to God for how he has worked in your life up to now.

Mark begins his Gospel by rooting it in God's promises and actions in the past. He also introduces several important themes that will be developed throughout the rest of the book. *Read Mark 1:1–13.*

---

1. What does verse 1 reveal about Mark's own view of the events he is about to describe?

2. Verses 2 and 3 combine quotations from Malachi and Isaiah about preparing the way for the coming of a king. Drawing together evidence from the whole passage, determine who is sending out his messenger (the "I" of v. 2).

Who does Mark suggest the coming king is?

Who is the messenger?

_____

3. What do you think it would be like to meet John?

_____

4. How does John's ministry prepare the way for Jesus?

_____

5. Malachi 4:5 describes this messenger as one having a ministry like that of the prophet Elijah. In 2 Kings 1:8 Elijah is described as a "man with a garment of hair and with a leather belt around his waist." Why do you think Mark includes the particular details he does about John's appearance (v. 6)?

_____

6. Malachi wrote more than 400 years before the coming of Jesus, and Isaiah wrote almost 400 years before Malachi. What difference does

it make to you that the gospel (the good news) is so deeply rooted in history?

7. What does the crowd's response to John's message suggest about their sense of need?

8. How does John emphasize the greatness of the one who will come after him (vv. 7–8)?

9. Despite his greatness Jesus came to John for baptism. What does this tell us about Jesus' relationship to us?

10. How do the events surrounding Jesus' baptism prepare him for his temptation in the desert?

11. Many of Mark's readers in Rome were facing wild animals in the arena under Nero's persecutions. How do you think they responded to Mark's description of Jesus' temptation (vv. 12–13)?

12. What encouragement do you find here for facing your own temptations?

*Ash God to help you find the strength and encouragement to face tempta-
tion. Ask him to prepare you more fully for the coming of the king as you
study Mark's Gospel.*

Now or Later

Read Malachi 3 and 4 carefully as a background to the ministry of John
and Jesus. What parallels can you find?

Make a study of 1 Kings 17–2 Kings 2 to see how John's ministry is
similar to Elijah's.

As you continue your study, ask yourself how Mark has set the scene
thus far for what's to come.

2

Portraits
of Jesus

We all live with authority—whether supervisors, professors, parents, police. And depending on how that authority is exercised, either we feel put upon, trapped and used, or we feel secure, free and useful.

GROUP DISCUSSION. Think of those who have authority over your life— parents, employer, teachers, the government. Is your response to their authority usually positive or negative? Explain why

PERSONAL REFLECTION. How do you respond to God's authority in your life—in fearful disregard, in grudging submission or in joyful obedience? How could a better understanding of Jesus' authority lead you to greater joy?

In 1:1–13 Mark has told us that Jesus has come as king to fulfill the Old Testament longings for the Lord's rule over all the earth. But what kind of king is he? Mark, it seems, knows that a picture is worth a thousand words. So rather than offering an abstract character analysis, he paints four verbal portraits of Jesus in action. *Read Mark 1:14–39.*

1. What do these four verbal portraits (16–20, 21–28, 29–34, 35–39) have in common?

___

2. We often think of the gospel solely as a message about the forgiveness of sins. What is the good news as Jesus proclaims it in verses 14–15?

___

3. What different factors contributed to the ready response of Simon and Andrew, James and John to Jesus' invitation (vv. 16–20)? (Don't forget 1:1–13!)

___

4. How does Jesus' command "follow me" summarize the essence of discipleship?

___

5. On the Sabbath Jesus goes to the synagogue (vv. 21–28). Imagine yourself there and describe what happens and how the people respond.

___

6. What might be some of the reasons that Jesus silences the demon from proclaiming who he is?

___

7. What impression of Jesus do you get from the portrait of his visit to the home of Simon and Andrew (vv. 29–34)?

8. How do the three portraits of Jesus' activity that we have looked at relate to his announcement in verse 15?

9. How does Jesus exercise his authority differently from kings and dictators and other human authorities?

10. What practical differences can knowing this make in your own response to Jesus' authority?

11. The quiet and solitude of verses 35–39 are quite a contrast from the previous events. What do these verses reveal about Jesus' priorities?

12. What steps do you need to take to bring your priorities more closely in line with his?

Ask God to open your eyes more widely to his servant-authority and to grant you joy in aligning your priorities more with his.

Now or Later

Jesus clearly felt the pull of conflicting needs. Yet in conversation with his Father he learned to establish priorities. Take some time to plan a schedule that will allow you to meet regularly with God in a "solitary place."

3

Friend of Outcasts

Mark 1:40–2:17

"Unclean! Unclean!" the man shouted, and everyone scattered to avoid contact with the leper—everyone except Jesus. We don't see a lot of lepers today—now they come in different shapes and sizes.

GROUP DISCUSSION. Have everyone in the group write on a slip of paper some type of person in our society that they feel uncomfortable with. Draw one of the slips and have some volunteers role play a chance meeting between this type of person and a group of Christians.

PERSONAL REFLECTION. Think of someone in the last few days or weeks who has made you uncomfortable. Try to identify just what you were reacting to and why.

The religious wisdom of Jesus' day demanded that a holy man keep away from various social outcasts, the "sinners." So Jesus was bound to encounter resistance as he openly welcomed them. This passage focuses on his compassion toward those we normally avoid. *Read Mark 1:40–2:17*, noticing how the pace slows down from 1:1–39.

1. As you look through the passage, what seem to be the main causes of the resistance Jesus faces?

2. Leviticus 13:45–46 states that a leper "must wear torn clothes, let his hair be unkempt, cover the lower part of his face and cry out, 'Unclean! Unclean!' As long as he has the infection he remains unclean. He must live alone; he must live outside the camp." Imagine yourself in his place. How would this disease affect you psychologically, religiously and socially?

3. What risks did the leper take in coming to Jesus (1:40–45)?

4. What risks did Jesus take in responding to him as he did?

5. How does Jesus respond to the man's total need?

6. Imagine that you are the paralytic being lowered before Jesus (2:1–12). How do you feel, especially when Jesus announces, "Son, your sins are forgiven"?

7. In what ways does Jesus' healing of the paralytic answer the questions raised in the minds of the teachers of the law?

8. The paralytic's friends provide a model of caring. What are some practical ways we can follow their example?

_____

9. Contrast the Pharisees' attitude toward tax collectors and "sinners" with Jesus' attitude.

_____

10. In his reply to the Pharisees' complaint about his eating with sinners and tax collectors, Jesus specifically compares himself to a doctor (2:17). How has he acted as a doctor throughout this passage?

_____

11. How is sin like illness, especially leprosy and paralysis?

_____

12. Jesus came announcing the kingdom and calling people to follow him. What change would need to take place in these Pharisees before they could answer Jesus' call?

_____

13. For the sake of God's kingdom, what steps can you take to reach out to today's "unlovely" or "unreachable"?

_____

Pray that God would give you eyes to see others as he does and to act toward them as he does.

Now or Later

Think of a group of "unreachable" or "disreputable" people that your church or small group could reach out to. Make a plan for ministering to them as whole people—with physical, social and psychological needs as well as religious needs. Put the plan into action.

4

Conflict
in Galilee

Mark 2:18–3:35

"A real Christian wouldn't do that." "Religion is fine, but you're becoming a fanatic!"

Such accusations are commonly leveled at Christians. They are difficult to bear under any circumstances. But when they come from family and friends, the pain is even greater.

GROUP DISCUSSION. What types of opposition have you encountered as a Christian? How has it made you feel?

PERSONAL REFLECTION. What is the most painful opposition you have encountered for Christ? Offer your pain to Jesus for his healing.

In the last study we saw the beginning of opposition to Jesus and his ministry. Now that opposition gains momentum, from the Pharisees and even Jesus' own family. This passage looks at some of the pressures and privileges of following Jesus. *Read Mark 2:18–3:35.*

1. On what grounds are Jesus and his disciples criticized in 2:18–3:6?

2. In 2:19–22, how does Jesus explain his disciples' failure to fast?

3. If you had been there, how would you have viewed the differences between Jesus' and the Pharisees' attitudes toward the Sabbath?

4. How do Jesus' comments in verses 27–28 rebuke both too rigid and too lax a view of the Sabbath?

5. What is ironic about the Pharisees' reaction to Jesus' healing on the Sabbath (3:1–6)?

6. The Pharisees objected to what Jesus and his disciples did and failed to do. What objections might people today have toward what we do or fail to do as Christians?

How can Jesus' responses to opposition be a model for our own responses?

7. While the Pharisees and the Herodians are plotting to kill Jesus, how are the common people responding to him (3:7–12)?

8. What charge do the teachers of the law bring against Jesus (3:22) and how does Jesus refute it (3:23–29)?

9. Jesus warns the teachers of the law about blaspheming against the Holy Spirit. How were they approaching the brink of total and unforgivable blindness to the truth?

10. Jesus' mother and brothers come for him because they think he is out of his mind (3:21, 31–32). How do you think this made Jesus feel?

11. When we are opposed or rejected by those who are closest to us, what comfort can we receive from Jesus' words in verses 33–35?

12. If we learn to see ourselves as part of God's family, rather than merely his slaves or subjects, how might that transform our attitude toward his commandments?

Offer prayers for strength and understanding in the face of opposition. Give thanks for being a part of God's family.

Now or Later

Look back at Jesus' original call to the fishermen in Mark 1:17. How do his plans for the twelve apostles in 3:14–15 fit with his original call?

What kind of king has Jesus shown himself to be thus far in Mark's Gospel?

What attracts you to him?

5

Kingdom Parables

Mark 4:1–34

Some stories wear their points on their sleeves, as it were. Others, to borrow from P. G. Wodehouse's definition of a parable, keep something up their sleeves "which suddenly pops up and knocks you flat."

GROUP DISCUSSION.   Mark Twain once said, "It's not the parts of the Bible I don't understand that bother me, but the parts I do understand!" Which parts of the Bible bother you more—the parts you understand or the parts you don't? Why?

PERSONAL REFLECTION.   What barriers in your life make it difficult for you to hear the voice of Jesus? Ask him to help you face and overcome them.

Among Jesus' stories we find a variety—from those that are easy to understand to those that are so difficult they invite our thought and reflection again and again. The stories in this passage contain vital information about God's kingdom and its subjects—for those who have ears to hear! *Read Mark 4:1–20*, watching especially for words and phrases that are repeated.

1. What idea or ideas seem to dominate verses 1–20?

_____

2. Jesus explains the parable of the sower (vv. 3–8) in verses 14–20. Put this explanation into your own words, describing from your experience examples of each kind of soil-seed combination.

_____

3. Verses 11–12 have long bothered many readers. The problem is that it looks like Jesus is saying that he tells parables to keep people from seeking forgiveness. From the context, which seems more likely—that verse 12 expresses the reason that Jesus speaks in parables or simply what happens when he does? Explain your answer.

_____

4. Notice that Jesus explains the parable of the soils to the disciples (vv. 10–12). What did they do to get an explanation that others did not?

_____

5. What does a willingness to ask indicate about a willingness to hear?

_____

6. On what grounds then are people included or excluded from the secret of the kingdom?

7. What is the secret of the kingdom? Be sure to make your case from evidence in the passage.

8. How does the response Jesus gets from telling the parable of the sower illustrate the point he is making?

9. What kind of soil are you?

What can you do to become the kind of soil Jesus is looking for?

10. The farmer was not being foolish in sowing the seed where he did. He was following the standard practice of the day—sowing then plowing. Only as time passed did each kind of soil reveal itself for what it was. What encouragement does this give you to "sow widely" as you share the good news of the kingdom with others?

11. What opportunities for sowing will you have this week?

Ask God to make you the kind of soil that serves his kingdom.

Now or Later

12. *Read Mark 4:21–34.* How do verses 21–25 help explain verses 11–12?

_____

13. What insights into kingdom growth do the parables of the growing seed and the mustard seed give us (vv. 26–34)?

_____

14. In this passage we see Jesus both spreading the message of the kingdom and teaching about how the kingdom grows. What lessons can we learn about evangelism both from his example and from his teaching?

Make plans to do some "sowing" activity with your small group or other Christian friends.

6

Fear & Faith

Mark 4:35–6:6

"Don't be afraid; just believe." These words may ring rather hollow when we, and not someone else, face a fearful or life-threatening situation. Yet in the face of real danger we discover just how much faith we have.

GROUP DISCUSSION.   Think of a time fear kept you from doing or saying something you thought you should. Explain how it felt and what you think you were really afraid of.

PERSONAL REFLECTION.   What fears inhibit you from sharing the gospel more readily with others? (Fear of rejection? fear you don't really know the gospel? something else?) Ask God to help you identify your fears and learn to overcome them with faith.

In this study we find a number of different people in desperate straits. Their experiences with Jesus can help us to trust him with the fearful areas of our own lives. *Read Mark 4:35–5:20.*

_____

1. In the first incident the disciples are quite naturally afraid of the storm and disturbed that Jesus seems unconcerned about their

drowning. Once Jesus calms the storm, however, they are still terrified. How does their fear after the storm differ from their previous fears?

_____

2. In 5:1–20 who is afraid and why?

_____

3. How do these fears compare with those in the previous incident (4:35–41)?

_____

4. Many people find it hard to understand why Jesus allowed the demons to destroy the pigs. It could have been to prevent a violent exit from the man or to show him visibly that he was now free. Even if we can't pin down exactly why Jesus allowed this, what does the fate of the pigs show about what the demons were trying to do to the man?

_____

5. What does this show about the value Jesus places on the man?

_____

6. At the end of this incident Jesus seems to reverse strategy For the first time he tells someone to go and tell others about his healing. How is this man different from the others? (See 1:21–26; 1:40–45; 3:7–12.)

7. *Read Mark 5:21–6:6*. In 5:21–43 two stories are woven together—the stories of Jairus's daughter and the woman with a hemorrhage. What sorts of fears are involved in these two incidents?

---

8. The word *fear* doesn't appear in the account of Jesus' return to his hometown, yet a kind of fear is evident here as well. What are the people afraid of?

---

9. Which of the different kinds of fear that have been described in these incidents might we label as good fears and which as bad?

---

10. What are the relationships between fear and faith in each of these incidents?

---

11. What keeps you from turning your fears into faith?

Offer your biggest fears to God and ask him to help you turn them into faith.

Now or Later

Study two (Mark 1:14–39) emphasized Jesus' authority over a similar array of life's experiences. What new dimensions of Jesus' authority are shown here?

How can this authority calm your fears and strengthen your faith?

Thinking back to the parable of the sower, what kinds of soil can you find in this passage?

7

Understanding the Loaves

Mark 6:6–52

Overactivity is all too common an experience among Christians today One of its most disastrous consequences is a hardened heart that keeps us from being refreshed by our Lord.

GROUP DISCUSSION. What in your life contributes to a sense of overactivity or burnout? How does it affect your spiritual life?

PERSONAL REFLECTION. Take a few minutes to assess the current state of your spiritual life. Is it fresh and vital? weak and mechanical? pressured? hardly there? Give thanks that the Lord cares about you wherever you are in your walk with him.

In this study we see the disciples suffering from overactivity and catch a vision of how Jesus can help us to counteract its effects. The passage we are focusing on is especially rich in Old Testament allusions. See if you can spot some of these allusions. *Read Mark 6:6–52.*

1. What do Jesus' instructions to the Twelve tell us about the kind of ministry they were to have (vv. 6–13)?

_____

2. What kind of man was Herod (vv. 14–29)?

_____

3. In terms of the parable of the sower, what kind of soil was he?

_____

4. This flashback to the execution of John the Baptist interrupts the account of Jesus' sending out the Twelve to preach and heal. Why do you suppose Mark recounts it here?

_____

5. What differences are there between Jesus' approach to the crowd and that of his disciples (vv. 30–44)?

_____

6. When has tiredness blunted your desire to care for others?

_____

7. Jesus and Herod, the two kings in this passage, both serve banquets. Compare the two.

8. Imagine yourself as one of the disciples in the boat (vv. 45–52). How would you respond to seeing Jesus walking on water?

9. What should the disciples have understood about the loaves (v. 52)?

10. Mark tells us that the disciples failed to understand the loaves because their hearts were hardened. What seems to have led to this hardness of heart?

11. Recognizing the contributing factors, what steps can we take to counteract overactivity and hardened hearts?

Offer prayers that God would hold you back from overactivity and keep his priorities before your eyes.

Now or Later

Take an extended time to be alone with God—a full Saturday morning or other convenient block of two or three hours. Spend some time journaling, noting what activities take up most of your time. Ask yourself and the Lord if these are the priorities he wants you to have. Are there people whose needs you are neglecting that you could make time for? Are there people who are taking up too much of your time that you need to cut back in seeing? Ask God for his discernment.

Study Ezekiel 34:1–16 to see how Mark 6:6–52 echoes God's judgment on the shepherds of Israel and his promise to become their shepherd himself.

8

Violating Tradition

Mark 6:53–7:37

All of us are influenced by traditions of one sort or another, even those of us who *by tradition* don't put much stock in them! But at what point do traditions lose their value or even become counterproductive? When do religious practices become a substitute for really obeying God?

GROUP DISCUSSION.   What religious traditions influence your life? Is that influence good or bad? Explain.

PERSONAL REFLECTION.   Make a list of three or four religious habits you have. Evaluate whether they help you to feel closer to God or whether they make you feel more distant.

In this study Jesus has some rather harsh words for the Pharisees and the traditions they choose to observe. See if you can discover the reason for his anger. *Read Mark 6:53–7:37.*

1. At the end of Mark 6 we see that as Jesus moves through the marketplace he goes about healing the sick. If you had been there, what

differences would you note about what the Pharisees do as they travel through the marketplace (7:1–4)?

2. What specific complaints does Jesus raise against the Pharisees' approach to tradition (7:6–13)?

3. What sorts of traditions do we observe today that get in the way of really honoring God?

4. How does Jesus' view of becoming "unclean" differ from that of the Pharisees (vv. 14–23)?

5. In what ways do we sometimes emphasize appearance over internal reality?

6. How does Jesus' standard of uncleanness cut across the differences between Jewish and Gentile traditions?

7. Jesus responds to the Syrophoenician woman's request with a mini–parable about children, bread and dogs (7:24–27). What is he actually saying?

8. What evidence is there that the woman has understood Jesus' point (vv. 28–30)?

_____

9. The healing of the deaf man takes place in the Decapolis, where Jesus has exorcised the demons from the Gerasene man at the tombs (5:1–20). How do the events here demonstrate the Gerasene man's success in telling about what Jesus had done for him (vv. 31–37)?

_____

10. What practical purposes do you think were served by Jesus' putting his fingers into the deaf man's ears and touching his tongue?

_____

11. Throughout Mark's Gospel physical ailments are seen to have spiritual counterparts. The deaf man in this account is obviously someone who quite literally has ears but is unable to hear or speak properly. In this chapter and the previous one, how do people exhibit symptoms of spiritual deafness?

_____

12. How can spiritual deafness separate us from God today?

Now, as then, those who are spiritually deaf—whether through hardness of heart or through substituting traditions for true obedience—can be healed by Jesus. Pray for yourself and others who need Jesus' healing touch.

Now or Later

Traditions by their very nature are hard to change. Is there one tradition in your church or fellowship group that more than any other inhibits the gospel? Work together to develop a strategy to address the problem.

9

Who Do You Say I Am?

Mark 8:1–9:1

"Who do you say I am?" It's a question Jesus asks each of us, and the answer we give ultimately determines our destiny But our answer involves more than what we say with our lips. Our real answer is to be found in the way we live our lives.

GROUP DISCUSSION. Ask each member of the group to think of a typical contemporary response to the question "Who is Jesus?" Role play roving reporter, asking each one, "Who do you think Jesus is?"

PERSONAL REFLECTION. C. S. Lewis made famous a set of contemporary alternative responses to Jesus' question—legend, liar, lunatic or Lord? In your heart of hearts, what is your response?

The whole Gospel of Mark so far has been supplying evidence for answering the question: Who is Jesus? Pay special attention as the events of this passage bring the first half of Mark's Gospel to a climax. *Read Mark 8:1–9:1.*

1. Why do you suppose the disciples, having witnessed the feeding of the 5,000, have such a hard time believing Jesus can supply the needs of 4,000 here (8:1–13)?

2. When have you acted similarly, not expecting God to work just after he has met a need in your life?

3. What details in Mark's account stress the adequacy of Jesus' ability to meet the people's needs?

4. In verse 12 Jesus says he will give no sign to this generation. What do you think he means in light of the many miraculous signs and healings he has already performed, not to mention his coming death and resurrection?

5. What is the yeast of the Pharisees and Herod (v. 15)? (For clues, look back to 6:14–29 and 7:1–23.)

6. What do the disciples fail to understand in verses 14–21 and why?

7. What unusual thing happens while Jesus is curing the blind man (vv. 22–26)?

8. In response to Jesus' question of who people are saying he is, the disciples tell him John the Baptist, Elijah or one of the prophets (vv. 27–30). Why would people think Jesus was any one of these?

_____

9. Right after Peter acknowledges Jesus to be the Christ, Jesus begins to explain what must happen to him. Why do you suppose Peter reacts so strongly to what Jesus has said?

_____

10. Why does Jesus respond to Peter so harshly?

_____

11. How is Peter like the blind man in verses 22–26?

_____

12. What does Jesus say it means to acknowledge him as the Christ and to follow him?

_____

13. Is your life characterized more by seeking to lose your life or to save it? Explain.

Ask Jesus to help you to see more clearly those areas where you are not yet following him.

Now or Later

If at all possible, I urge you to take a whole session to work through the following review of Mark 1–8. The truth about Jesus has progressively unfolded. With Peter's confession in 8:29 we reach not only the midpoint but also a key turning point in Mark's Gospel. For this reason it is especially useful to review some of the key themes developed thus far.

1. What are some of the things Mark has most emphasized about Jesus?

2. What key things have been revealed about his kingdom?

3. Go back through each study so far and retitle it to show how it fits in with the kingdom theme. For example, study one could be titled "The Coming of the Promised King."

4. How can we make the message of the king and his kingdom a more vital part of our proclaiming the good news?

5. What have we observed about Jesus as a communicator of the gospel?

6. How can this improve the way we communicate the gospel?

7. Throughout the early chapters of Mark, Jesus seems cautious about revealing his identity too quickly. Why do you think this is so?

---

8. In the parable of the sower we first confront the problem of hearing. Jesus talks about the failure of the path, the rocky soil and the thorn–infested soil to produce fruit. As we move on, we begin to see that even the disciples have difficulty hearing and seeing because their hearts are hardened. How is this problem—the hardened heart, the blind eyes and the deaf ears—to be solved?

---

9. What are some areas where you have begun to see more clearly and to hear with a more responsive heart?

10

Suffering & Glory

Mark 9:2–32

In a famous short story the main character is given the choice of opening one of two doors. Behind one is a beautiful maiden; behind the other, a ferocious tiger. It is easy to identify with the hero of the story, hoping for joy rather than suffering, pleasure rather than pain. But what if we cannot have one without the other?

GROUP DISCUSSION. What sort of suffering in relation to the gospel do you most fear? Why?

PERSONAL REFLECTION. When has fear of some kind of suffering kept you from sharing or embracing the gospel? Tell Jesus how that makes you feel.

The passage in this study examines the relationship between suffering and glory, human weakness and divine power. *Read Mark 9:2–32.*

1. Put yourself in the place of Peter, James and John in verses 1–12. What do you see and hear?

As a good Jew, what significance might you have attached to the presence of Elijah and Moses with Jesus on the mount?

2. Jesus' transfiguration occurs six days after Jesus said, "I tell you the truth, some who are standing here will not taste death before they see the kingdom of God come with power" (9:1). What connection do you see between the transfiguration and Jesus' promise?

3. The statement in verse 7, "Listen to him!" probably alludes to Deuteronomy 18:14–22. How can we listen to Jesus today?

4. To what events is Jesus referring when he says, "Elijah has come, and they have done to him everything they wished, just as it is written about him" (v. 13)?

5. Elijah's return was expected to immediately precede the inauguration of the glorious messianic kingdom (Malachi 4:5). Yet how is what happened to him (v. 13) a pattern for what must also happen to Jesus (vv. 9, 12) and to us?

6. Jesus descends the mountain and returns to his other disciples only to find them in hot debate with the teachers of the law over their failure to exorcise a young boy robbed of speech (vv. 14–18). Why do you

suppose Jesus is so harsh in verse 19?

---

7. Think back to the leper in chapter 1. How is the father's request in verse 22 similar to and yet different from the leper's request in 1:40?

---

8. Which do you struggle with more—believing that Jesus can or that he wants to answer your prayers? Explain.

---

9. How can the dialogue between Jesus and the man encourage you when your faith is weak?

---

10. At the end of this account Jesus again tells his disciples about his death and resurrection (vv. 30–32). Why do you suppose the disciples failed to understand what he meant?

---

11. What details in the account of the boy's healing parallel those in Jesus' prediction of his coming suffering and victory?

---

12. How can this passage encourage us in the midst of pain and suffering?

Pray for God's strength to face pain and suffering.

Now or Later

Read the story of Elijah's encounter with Ahab and the prophets of Baal in 1 Kings 18:1–19:18. How is Elijah called on to face suffering for doing the Lord's work?

How does God empower him?

Even after his success Elijah feels like a failure. How does God care for him then?

Elijah's counterpart, John the Baptist, is not so fortunate—his faithfulness ends in death (Mark 6:14–29). How do you reconcile his fate with the promise of God's faithfulness?

What added perspective does Jesus' death shed on this issue?

11

The First
& the Last

Mark 9:33–50

All of us, I imagine, struggle with the question of status and identity within a group. Where do I fit? How important am I to this group? Who is on our side? Who isn't?

GROUP DISCUSSION.   How would you define success? Would you say you've achieved it?

PERSONAL REFLECTION.   Think of a rival at work or in a group you're involved in. How do you typically respond to that person? Ask God to help you see that person as he does.

In this study we find out how Jesus turns conventional wisdom about status and group identity on its ear. *Read Mark 9:33–50.*

1. In verses 33–37, what is Jesus trying to get across to the disciples?

2. Thinking back through all the Gospel of Mark to this point, how

have we seen this principle of the first and the last in action?

___

3. Why is a child so appropriate an illustration for Jesus' point?

___

4. What attitudes (that we all share) motivate John's remarks in verse 38?

___

5. What perspective governs Jesus' response to John in verses 39–41?

___

6. What further rebuke to John is given in verses 42–50?

___

7. How are Jesus' attitudes about greatness and personal worth radically different from attitudes we often adopt from society?

___

8. Christian history has known some individuals to take Jesus' words in verses 43–47 quite literally. Why is cutting off a hand or foot or plucking out an eye not radical enough a way to deal with sin?

___

9. Verse 49 is somewhat of a mixed metaphor, but fire has been used as

an image in verses 42–48. Taking a cue from 42–48, what do you think it means to be "salted with fire"?

10. If salt is connected with fire as an image of judgment, what do you think having salt in yourself might mean?

How would that contribute to peace?

11. What individuals or groups are we tempted to silence because they are not one of us?

12. Does this mean we shouldn't oppose anyone, or does Jesus give limits?

13. What attitudes and actions does this passage suggest should govern our relationships with rival individuals or groups who act in Jesus' name?

Pray for unity and a sense of common purpose among Christians and Christian groups you know.

Now or Later

Make plans to join together in worship or an evangelistic outreach with another church or Christian group where you live.

12

New
Relationships

Mark 10:1–31

For many of us preachin' becomes meddlin' when it impinges on how we live. But Jesus and the New Testament, like the Old Testament before them, never allow religion to be divorced from family life and social relationships.

GROUP DISCUSSION. Churches have been criticized both for being too lax and for being too strict about divorce. How would you describe your church's stand on divorce?

PERSONAL REFLECTION. How has the Christian community been (or not been) a family to you?

This passage for this study exposes some of the ways the gospel ought to transform our family and social lives. *Read Mark 10:1–31.*

1. What common themes do you see running through this passage?

2. What differences in approach to the question of divorce seem evident between Jesus and the Pharisees?

3. On the basis of verses 6–9 some Christian churches have refused to recognize divorce even when a couple has obtained a civil dissolution of their marriage. Do you think this is the intent of Jesus' statement? Why or why not?

4. In a culture which granted far more freedom to men than to women, what significant further statements on divorce does Jesus make in verses 11–12?

5. In verses 13–16 we find that Jesus has used a child or children for the second time to illustrate a spiritual principle. What does it mean to receive the kingdom like a little child?

6. In what ways do you think the expectations of the rich man about how Jesus would answer his question in verse 17 differed from Jesus' response in verses 18–21?

7. Why is it so hard for the rich to enter the kingdom (vv. 22–27)?

8. What obstacles were or are hardest for you to overcome in entering the kingdom?

How has God helped you?

9. How have the Pharisees (vv. 2–9) and the rich man (vv. 17–25) failed to receive the kingdom like a child (v. 15)?

10. In what areas of your life do you most need to express more childlike faith in God?

11. What does Peter seem to be getting at by his comments in verse 28?

12. How does Jesus reassure Peter?

13. How have you experienced the truth of Jesus' words here?

Pray to learn to receive the kingdom as a little child.

Now or Later

Reflect in prayer and/or in a journal about being a child before God. What characteristics of a child do you think God wants us to emulate? How are you like and not like a child? What does it mean to you that God wants to be your parent?

13

Blindness & Sight

Mark 10:32–52

The blind sometimes have uncanny "sight," and the deaf sometimes "hear" what others miss. Spiritual insight and alertness arise from the heart rather than from status or position.

GROUP DISCUSSION. What do you think are some of the privileges and responsibilities of a leader?

PERSONAL REFLECTION. What are some spiritual truths that God has allowed you to see and hear? Give thanks for what you know of him.

In this passage Mark seems to delight in the irony of a blind man who perceives what the sighted cannot see. *Read Mark 10:32–52.*

1. In verses 32–34 Jesus predicts his death for a third time. Compare this prediction with the previous two (8:31; 9:31). What do you observe?

2. Given what Jesus has just said, what is ironic about James and John's request (vv. 35–37)?

3. What seems to motivate James and John's request?

4. Why do you think they go about asking the way they do?

5. What does Jesus mean by the cup he is to drink and the baptism he is to be baptized with (vv. 38–39)?

6. When the other ten apostles hear about this status request, they become indignant. In response, Jesus again emphasizes that the last will be first. What new motivation for service is found in verse 45?

7. How can your life better conform to Jesus' view of greatness? (Consider what motivates your actions as well as what you do.)

8. From the brief account in verses 46–52, what kind of man does Bartimaeus seem to be?

9. Why do you suppose Jesus asked Bartimaeus what he wanted him to do for him?

_____

10. Once Jesus heals him, Bartimaeus sets out to follow Jesus along the road to Jerusalem. What might it mean for Bartimaeus to be on this road with Jesus (10:32–34)?

_____

11. What has Bartimaeus seen that the disciples have not?

_____

12. Jesus is indeed on the road to glory, but that road will not bypass Jerusalem. Self-sacrifice and service mark the way What are some present opportunities for you to follow Jesus?

What may be some of the costs?

Pray that Jesus will help you to be ready to pay the costs of following him.

Now or Later

Do some journal reflection on the costs of following Jesus. What do you sense are his priorities for you right now? Who does he want you to reach out to? What will it cost you in time and energy to follow through on these priorities?

14

Palm Sunday

Mark 11:1–25

The trouble with righteous anger is that it is so much easier to be angry than righteous. But it is possible to be both.

GROUP DISCUSSION. How would you define righteous anger? When have you seen it put to good use?

PERSONAL REFLECTION. When has anger got the better of you lately? Ask God to help you discern the real cause of the anger.

Jesus well illustrates righteous anger in this passage. He also suggests that even righteous anger must be joined with prayer and forgiveness. This passage provides an example of how our emotions and attitudes can work toward God's purposes instead of against them. *Read Mark 11:1–25.*

1. What progression of moods do you see in this passage?

2. In what ways is the significance of Jesus' entry into Jerusalem reinforced?

3. Put yourself in Jesus' place. Why is he so angry with what is taking place in the temple (vv. 15–17)?

4. Are there similar activities or attitudes in your church or fellowship which get in the way of God's purposes?

What can you do to help eliminate them?

5. Why do you suppose Mark has sandwiched this account of Jesus' clearing out of the temple within that of the cursing of the fig tree?

6. What kind of fruit was Jesus looking for in Israel?

7. Many people believe they will escape the judgment of God simply because they are religious. How can this passage serve as a warning to them and to us?

8. What does Jesus teach us about prayer in verses 23–25?

9. Jesus may have been speaking about praying for the day of judgment in verse 23. If praying to move mountains is praying for the day of God's judgment, why is it important to pray with the attitude Jesus describes in verse 25?

10. Thinking back to your response to question 4, are there any people you need to forgive as well as to rebuke?

11. Is there anything else you need to do to be reconciled to this person or persons? If so, how and when will you do it?

Respond to this passage in prayer, praising the King of peace and asking that his kingdom might be established.

Now or Later
Study Zechariah 14 to see in what ways Mark makes use of Zechariah's imagery to describe the coming "day of the Lord." Read Zechariah 9:9–10 on the triumphal entry into Jerusalem.

15

Tempting Questions

Mark 11:27–12:27

Some people ask questions because they want to know the answers. Others take malicious delight in posing unanswerable questions or in trying to trip up an opponent. Jesus often asked questions to get his hearers to think deeply for themselves.

GROUP DISCUSSION. Tell about one of the hardest questions someone has asked you. How did you respond?

PERSONAL REFLECTION. Think of a friend who asks you really tough questions about the faith. Can you see any deeper questions behind the questions he or she asks?

Learning to look behind questions to motives and learning to pose effective questions can help us all to be better evangelists and servants. *Read Mark 11:27–12:27.*

1. What are some of the motives behind the questions that are asked

throughout the passage?

2. In 11:27 the chief priests, the elders and the teachers of the law come asking a seemingly straightforward question about Jesus' authority What does Jesus' reply and the subsequent discussion reveal about their motives?

3. Why doesn't Jesus answer them?

4. Are there times when we shouldn't answer questioners? Explain.

5. Focus on 12:1–12. If the tenants are Israel and its religious leaders, who are the owner, the servants and the son?

6. How are these religious leaders about to fulfil the Scripture Jesus cites in 12:10–11?

7. A common enemy can often draw together people who are not otherwise on good terms. In 12:13–17 we find Herodians (supporters of the puppet monarchy) and the Pharisees (ardent nationalists and

opponents of Roman rule) joining forces. How does the question they pose to Jesus reflect their conflicting interests?

8. Jesus not only avoids their trap by his answer, he also succeeds in establishing an important principle. What sorts of things are rightfully Caesar's (the government's) and what are God's?

9. The Sadducees differed from their Jewish contemporaries because they rejected the idea of resurrection. What motives lie behind their question to Jesus (12:18–23)?

10. How is Jesus' response from Scripture particularly appropriate for the Sadducees who accepted only the authority of the Pentateuch (the first five books of the Old Testament)?

11. How are you experiencing the truth of the Scriptures and the power of God?

12. How can we get to know the Scriptures and the power of God better?

13. As we seek to share the good news of Jesus and his kingdom, we will meet people with a wide variety of questions and motives. What can we learn about answering and asking questions from this passage?

Pray that God will make you an effective poser and answerer of questions.

Now or Later

Develop your own list of common questions people ask, using parallel columns for possible questions behind the questions. Then fill in possible responses. If you are studying with a group, role play to practice responding to a variety of these questions.

16

An End to Questions

Mark 12:28–44

People are motivated by many things—ambition, money, power, recognition, the desire to please God.

GROUP DISCUSSION. What do you see as the most powerful motivations in people's lives around you?

PERSONAL REFLECTION. What motivates your daily life and future plans?

In the passage for this study Jesus encounters or comments on a variety of people whose lives are governed by different goals. In so doing he exposes our own motivations to his searching glance. *Read Mark 12:28–44.*

1. Like the chief priests, elders, Pharisees and Sadducees of 11:27–12:27, another teacher of the law comes to Jesus with a pointed question (v. 28). What evidence is there that he is not out to trap Jesus?

2. Though Jesus is only asked for one commandment (Deuteronomy 6:4–5), in good rabbinic fashion he responds by adding a second to his reply (Leviticus 19:18). What relationship does this second commandment bear to the first?

3. The teacher not only endorses Jesus' answer, he takes it a step further. What are some contemporary examples of burnt offerings and sacrifices?

4. If you were to evaluate your daily activities on the basis of love for God and neighbour, how would you fare? Explain.

5. What steps can you take to make the love of God and love of neighbour a higher priority in your life?

6. How has Jesus succeeded in silencing his questioners? (Look back over 11:27–12:34 to answer this.)

7. To a Jew in Jesus' day a descendant was always inferior to an ancestor. A son might call his father or grandfather "lord" but never vice versa. How can the Christ be both David's Lord and his descendant (vv. 35–37)?

8. What does it mean for us to call Jesus "Lord"?

_____

9. What warning to us is present in Jesus' cautions about the teachers of the law (vv. 38–40)?

_____

10. In contrast to the teachers of the law and the rich, what motivates the widow's religious behaviour?

_____

11. How does she fulfil the great commandment?

_____

12. What implications does this example have for our giving to the Lord's work?

_____

Ask God to give you the attitude of the widow both in your love for him and toward others.

Now or Later

Read Malachi 3:1–5. In what ways has Jesus been fulfilling this prophecy in Mark 11–12?

17

Keep Watch

Waiting for Christmas can keep some children excited and on their best behavior for weeks. But what if Christmas never came? To many of us the second coming of Christ may seem like a Christmas that never comes.

GROUP DISCUSSION. Why do you think so many of us have such a fascination with the future?

PERSONAL REFLECTION. How do you feel about the Lord's return? Is it something you look forward to, dread or don't think about? Why?

In this passage Jesus answers some questions about the future, both near and far off, but above all he encourages an attitude we all need to develop. *Read Mark 13:1–37.*

1. From the context, what are Peter, James, John and Andrew asking about in verse 4?

2. Jesus doesn't seem to answer their question directly, at least not at first. What is he concerned about?

3. How would Jesus' warnings and encouragements (vv. 5–13) have helped the disciples in the early years of the church?

4. What relevance do these warnings and encouragements have for us today?

5. Christians have sometimes disagreed about how to interpret Jesus' words in verses 14–23. Some think Jesus is talking about the destruction of the temple in A.D. 70 and the events leading up to that. Others think these events are still future. What evidence is there to support each view?

6. What does Jesus say about God's work in the midst of all this turmoil?

7. How is the distress described in verses 24–27 different from that described in verses 5–23?

8. How would verses 26–27 encourage those who have experienced the

distress preceding Jesus' return?

9. Six times Jesus warns his disciples to "watch, be on guard" (vv. 5, 9, 23, 33, 35, 37). Why?

10. Many people throughout the ages have tried to make precise predictions about the return of Jesus. How does watching as Jesus urges differ from making such predictions?

11. In what practical ways can we be alert for Jesus' return?

Pray that you might be alert and ready for Jesus' return.

Now or Later

Make a careful comparison of Mark's account of Jesus' teaching here with Matthew's (24–25) and Luke's (21:5–38). What do they have in common?

What unique features do you find in each?

How do they all encourage us to prepare for Jesus' return?

18

The Betrayer Approaches

Mark 14:1–42

Have you ever fallen asleep in a public place—in a meeting at work? during the sermon at church? Or have you ever found yourself yawning just when you were trying to be especially attentive to someone?

GROUP DISCUSSION. Tell a story about a time you fell asleep at a critical or embarrassing time.

PERSONAL REFLECTION. In what areas of your life do you feel that your spirit is willing but your flesh is weak? Ask the Lord to begin strengthening you in that area.

In this study we enter clearly into the last few days of Jesus' earthly ministry. The mood is somber as more and more people begin to fail and desert him. Try to empathize with Jesus as you read. *Read Mark 14:1–42.*

---

1. Imagine you were with Jesus throughout these events. How do the mood and activities change from what takes place in verses 1–9 to what

takes place in verses 10–42?

2. What different motives are present in the conflict that arises at the home of Simon the leper?

3. How might Jesus' own teaching have prompted the response of the objectors?

4. The woman's act is in one sense an act of worship. What light, if any, does this incident shed on the competing claims for beauty in worship and concern for the poor?

5. During the Passover feast Jesus tells the Twelve that one of them will betray him. What do you think they were feeling as they responded to his announcement (v. 19)?

6. Few words have spawned as much debate regarding their meaning as those Jesus spoke in verses 22–24. Regardless of how literally we take them, what are the bread and cup of the Lord's Supper to symbolize for us?

7. In verse 27 Jesus predicts that his disciples will desert him under pressure. How do you empathize (or fail to empathize) with Peter's assertions in verses 29–31?

---

8. Many people question whether the only way to God is through Jesus and his death on the cross. Edith Schaeffer has suggested that this is the question Jesus himself wrestled with in Gethsemane (vv. 35–36). How might this passage help those who struggle with the question of whether Jesus is the only way to God?

---

9. In verse 34 and again in verse 38 Jesus encourages the disciples to watch and pray so that they not fall into temptation. What particular temptations were they about to face?

How might prayer have changed the outcome?

---

10. How can these same exhortations make the difference in your own life between resisting or falling into temptation?

---

11. Have you ever felt like the disciples must have felt in verse 40? Explain.

12. What consolation and encouragement can you draw from the disciples' experience?

Pray that the Lord will strengthen you in times when you are struggling to keep following him.

Now or Later

Read up on the issue of whether Jesus is the only way. Some good places to start are Mark Ashton's *Absolute Truth?* (InterVarsity Press, 1996), Douglas Groothuis's *Are All Religions One?* (InterVarsity Press, 1996), Peter Kreeft and Ronald K. Tacelli's *Handbook of Christian Apologetics* (InterVarsity Press, 1994) and Norman Anderson's *Christianity and World Religions* (InterVarsity Press, 1984).

19

Betrayed!

The persecution of enemies is one thing, the abandonment of friends another.

GROUP DISCUSSION. What does being loyal to a friend mean to you?

PERSONAL REFLECTION. What pressures do you feel that test your loyalty to Jesus Christ? Tell him what you're feeling.

In this study we find Jesus not only betrayed by one of his disciples but abandoned by all the others and ruefully denied by one of his closest friends. All this added to the cruel and unlawful treatment by the Sanhedrin. This account reveals how intense pressures can test the quality of our discipleship. *Read Mark 14:43–72.*

---

1. What mixed motives do you see among the main characters in this passage?

In particular, what mixed motives may have inspired Judas's words and action of betrayal (vv. 43–45)?

2. How does Jesus respond to his betrayal (vv. 48–49)?

3. The unnamed young man seems symbolic of all Jesus' followers. How does his predicament reflect Jesus' warnings about the cost of discipleship (8:34–38)?

4. What aspects of Jesus' trial before the Sanhedrin does Mark emphasize?

5. Up until this point Jesus has regularly disguised his identity, but in verse 62 he openly confesses his identity as the Christ. Why do you think he does this now?

6. How is the charge against Jesus (v. 64) both justifiable and unjustifiable?

7. How is Jesus, in contrast to his disciples, an example of the kind of discipleship he desires in us (vv. 55–65)?

8. What mix of motives brings Peter into the high priest's courtyard yet keeps him from acknowledging his relationship to Jesus (vv. 66–72)?

_____

9. How are your motives mixed in following Jesus?

_____

10. How is Judas's betrayal of Jesus different from Peter's?

_____

11. In what circumstances are you most tempted to be ashamed of Jesus or to deny him?

_____

12. What warnings and encouragement can you draw from Peter's experience?

Ask the Lord to sort out your motives and help you to be faithful to him.

Now or Later

Imagine yourself to be Peter or one of the other twelve apostles. Read slowly and reflectively through Mark 14:1–15:47. Record in a journal what it's like to watch Jesus go through his betrayal, arrest, trial, death and burial. Then read Mark 16:1–8 and record what it's like to find him alive again. What impact would this have on your life?

20

Victory Snatched from Defeat

Mark 15–16

True greatness, Jesus taught, is found in being a servant: "Whoever wants to be first must be slave of all. For even the Son of Man did not come to be served, but to serve, and to give his life as a ransom for many."

GENERAL DISCUSSION. Share responses to either of these two questions: (1) What does the world consider true greatness to be? (2) In the eyes of the world, was Jesus truly a great man? Why or why not?

PERSONAL REFLECTION. Take time to reflect on what it was like for Jesus to face his own death. Give thanks to him for his willingness to go through it for you.

Recorded here is the vivid testimony to Jesus' greatness and glory. *Read Mark 15:1–16:8.*

1. What kind of man is Pilate (15:1–15)?

_____

2. What evidence is there that he wants to do what is right?

_____

3. What keeps him from doing what is right?

_____

4. How can we keep from succumbing to the same temptation?

_____

5. In what sense is Barabbas a stand-in for every believer?

_____

6. The wine mixed with myrrh offered to Jesus would have had a narcotic effect. Why does Jesus refuse it? (See 10:38; 14:25, 36.)

_____

7. What ironies are present in the charges and jeers directed toward Jesus on the cross (15:25–32)?

_____

8. In what ways is the centurion's confession a climax to the whole of

Mark's Gospel? (Compare 15:38–39 with 1:1, 10–11; 8:28–30.)

9. Why do you think it was Joseph and the women who had followed Jesus, and not the eleven, who were present when Jesus died and his body needed a tomb?

10. Why is it significant that Peter is mentioned by name in 16:7?

11. What reassurance can we draw from the Lord's evident forgiveness of Peter (see 3:28)?

12. The earliest and best manuscripts of Mark's Gospel end at 16:8. Nearly all scholars agree that if Mark did not end his work here, we have lost what he wrote (vv. 9–20 were clearly written by someone else). While some still hold that the original ending has been lost, many scholars believe Mark intended to end with verse 8 as it is. How is verse 8 an appropriate ending to the gospel story?

13. How can this passage reinforce our commitment to sharing the good news of Christ with others?

Give thanks to Jesus for his willingness to go to the cross and for his glorious resurrection.

Now or Later.

If possible, I urge you to take a whole session to work through the following review of Mark 9–16.

New light brings new responsibility. Now that you have concluded your study of Mark, how will your life be different? This final study reviews some of the central themes of Mark's Gospel and reminds us of how they are to affect our lives.

---

1. What have you learned about Mark as a writer and an evangelist?

---

2. How has your understanding of the gospel and the kingdom been enriched?

---

3. The disciples' performance in this half of Mark's Gospel has been almost entirely marked by failure (9:18–19; 10:35–45; 14:32–42, 43–52, 66–72). Review the specific instances of failure and then explain why Mark may have drawn so much attention to them.

What can we learn from this?

---

4. Many scholars believe one of Mark's purposes in writing his account of Jesus' ministry was to counteract a misconception about Jesus

himself and the Christian life. Some Christians tended to emphasize Jesus as a glorious, other–worldly figure to the exclusion of his humanity and suffering. As a result, they expected to be spared suffering in this life and to quickly join Jesus in the glories of heaven. Unfortunately, many Christians today share this view of the Christian life. How does Mark systematically undercut this view? (Be sure to consider the themes of following Christ, the cost of discipleship and the road to glory.)

5. Where in Mark's account is Jesus' glory most prominently displayed? Give reasons to support your answer.

6. How might the cross fulfill Jesus' words in 9:1, at least in part?

7. If the path to glory is marked by discipline, suffering and servanthood, how will your life need to change?

How will your sharing of the gospel need to change?

8. What did you appreciate most about your study of Mark?

Leader's Notes

MY GRACE IS SUFFICIENT FOR YOU. (2 COR 12:9)

Leading a Bible discussion can be an enjoyable and rewarding experience. But it can also be scary, especially if you've never done it before. If this is your feeling, you're in good company. When God asked Moses to lead the Israelites out of Egypt, he replied, "O Lord, please send someone else to do it!" (Ex 4:13). It was the same with Solomon, Jeremiah and Timothy, but God helped these people in spite of their weaknesses, and he will help you as well.

You don't need to be an expert on the Bible or a trained teacher to lead a Bible discussion. The idea behind these inductive studies is that the leader guides group members to discover for themselves what the Bible has to say. This method of learning will allow group members to remember much more of what is said than a lecture would.

These studies are designed to be led easily. As a matter of fact, the flow of questions through the passage, from observation to interpretation to application, is so natural that you may feel the studies lead themselves. This study guide is also flexible. You can use it with a variety of groups—student, professional, neighbourhood or church groups. Each study takes forty–five to sixty minutes in a group setting.

There are some important facts to know about group dynamics and encouraging discussion. The suggestions listed below should enable you to fulfil your role as leader effectively and enjoyably.

Preparing for the Study

1. Ask God to help you understand and apply the passage in your own life.
   Unless this happens, you will not be prepared to lead others. Pray too for

the various members of the group. Ask God to open your hearts to the message of his Word and motivate you to action.

2. Read the introduction to the guide to get an overview of the entire book and the issues that will be explored.

3. As you begin each study, read and reread the assigned Bible passage to familiarize yourself with it.

4. This study guide is based on the New International Version of the Bible. It will help you and the group if you use this translation as the basis for your study and discussion.

5. Carefully work through each question in the study. Spend time in meditation and reflection as you consider how to respond.

6. Write your thoughts and responses in the space provided in the study guide. This will help you to express your understanding of the passage clearly.

7. It might help to have a Bible dictionary handy. Use it to look up any unfamiliar words, names or places. (For additional help on how to study a passage, see chapter five of *How to Lead a LifeBuilder Study*, IVP, 2018.)

8. Consider how you can apply the Scripture to your life. Remember that the group will follow your lead in responding to the studies. They will not go any deeper than you do.

9. Once you have finished your own study of the passage, familiarize yourself with the leader's notes for the study you are leading. These are designed to help you in several ways. First, they tell you the purpose the study guide author had in mind when writing the study. Take time to think through how the study questions work together to accomplish that purpose. Second, the notes provide you with additional background information or suggestions on group dynamics for various questions. This information can be useful if people have difculty understanding or answering a question. Third, the leader's notes can alert you to potential problems you may encounter during the study.

10. If you wish to remind yourself of anything mentioned in the leader's notes, make a note to yourself below that question in the study.

Leading the Study

1. Begin the study on time. Open with prayer, asking God to help the group understand and apply the passage.

2. Be sure that everyone in your group has a study guide. Encourage the group to prepare beforehand for each discussion by reading the introduction to the guide and by working through the questions in the study.

3. At the beginning of your first time together, explain that these studies are meant to be discussions, not lectures. Encourage the members of the group to participate. However, do not put pressure on those who may be hesitant to speak during the first few sessions. You may want to suggest the following guidelines to your group.

   - Stick to the topic being discussed.

   - Your responses should be based on the verses which are the focus of the discussion and not on outside authorities such as commentaries or speakers.

   - These studies focus on a particular passage of Scripture. Only rarely should you refer to other portions of the Bible. This allows for everyone to participate in in–depth study on equal ground.

   - Anything said in the group is considered confidential and will not be discussed outside the group unless specific permission is given to do so.

   - We will listen attentively to each other and provide time for each person present to talk.

   - We will pray for each other.

4. Have a group member read the introduction at the beginning of the discussion.

5. Every session begins with a group discussion question. The question or activity is meant to be used before the passage is read. The question introduces the theme of the study and encourages group members to begin to open up. Encourage as many members as possible to participate and be ready to get the discussion going with your own response.

   This section is designed to reveal where our thoughts or feelings need to be transformed by Scripture. That is why it is especially important not to read the passage before the discussion question is asked. The passage will tend to color the honest reactions people would otherwise give because they are, of course, supposed to think the way the Bible does.

   You may want to supplement the group discussion question with an ice-breaker to help people to get comfortable. See the community section of the *Small Group Starter Kit* (IVP, 1995) for more ideas.

You also might want to use the personal reflection question with your group. Either allow a time of silence for people to respond individually or discuss it together.

6. Have a group member (or members if the passage is long) read aloud the passage to be studied. Then give people several minutes to read the passage again silently so that they can take it all in.

7. Question 1 will generally be an overview question designed to briefly survey the passage. Encourage the group to do this, but try to avoid getting sidetracked by questions or issues that will be addressed later in the study.

8. As you ask the questions, keep in mind that they are designed to be used just as they are written. You may simply read them aloud, or you may prefer to express them in your own words.

   There may be times when it is appropriate to deviate from the study guide. For example, a question may have already been answered. If so, move on to the next. Or someone may raise an important question not covered in the guide. Take time to discuss it, but try to keep the group from going off at a tangent.

9. Avoid answering your own questions. If necessary, repeat or rephrase them until they are clearly understood, or point out something you have read in the leader's notes to clarify the context or meaning. An eager group quickly becomes passive and silent if they think the leader will do most of the talking.

10. Don't be afraid of silence. People may need time to think about the question before formulating their answers.

11. Don't be content with just one answer. Ask, "What do the rest of you think?" or "Anything else?" until several people have given answers to the question.

12. Acknowledge all contributions. Try to be afrming whenever possible. Never reject an answer. If it is clearly off-base, ask, "Which verse led you to that conclusion?" or again, "What do the rest of you think?"

13. Don't expect every answer to be addressed to you, even though this will probably happen at first. As group members become more at ease, they will begin to truly interact with each other. This is one sign of healthy discussion.

14. Don't be afraid of controversy. It can be very stimulating. If you don't resolve an issue completely, don't be frustrated. Move on and keep it in mind for later. A subsequent study may solve the problem.

15. Periodically summarize what the group has said about the passage. This helps to draw together the various ideas mentioned and gives continuity to the study. But don't preach.

16. At the end of the Bible discussion you may want to allow group members a time of quiet to work on an idea under "Now or Later." Then discuss what you experienced. Or you may want to encourage group members to work on these ideas between meetings. Give an opportunity during the session to allow people to talk about what they are learning.

17. Conclude your time together with conversational prayer, adapting the prayer suggestion at the end of the study to your group. Ask for God's help in following through on the commitments you have made.

18. End on time.

Many more suggestions and helps are found in *How to Lead a LifeBuilder Study*.

Components of Small Groups

A healthy small group should do more than study the Bible. There are four components to consider as you structure your time together.

Nurture. Small groups help us to grow in our knowledge and love of God. Bible study is the key to making this happen and is the foundation of your small group.

Community. Small groups are a great place to develop deep friendships with other Christians. Allow time for informal interaction before and after each study. Plan activities and games that will help you get to know each other. Spend time having fun—going on a picnic or cooking dinner together.

Worship and prayer. Your study will be enhanced by spending time praising God together in prayer or song. Pray for each other's needs, and keep track of how God is answering prayer in your group. Ask God to help you apply what you are learning in your study.

Outreach. Reaching out to others can be a practical way of applying what you are learning, and it will keep your group from becoming self–focused. Host a series of evangelistic discussions for your friends or neighbors. Clean up the yard of an elderly friend. Serve at a soup kitchen together, or spend a day working in the community.

Many more suggestions and helps in each of these areas are found in the *Small Group Starter Kit*. You will also find information on building a small group. Reading through the starter kit will be worth your time.

The Big Picture

In any set of studies covering a whole book like Mark, there is an inevitable trade–off between giving attention to details and getting the big picture. If these studies err on one side or the other, they err on the side of trying to see the big picture. Thus some passages may seem a little long, but they have a unified theme. In the revision process for this second edition, most of the Old Testament background exploration has been moved to the "Now or Later" section, as have some of the questions that tie together observations from previous studies.

I think the effort to see the Gospel as a whole, rather than as a set of isolated units, will be richly rewarding. But it will require discipline on the part of leader and group members together to press on and not get bogged down in details.

Part 1: Who Is Jesus? Mark 1–8

Study 1. Mark 1:1–13. Gospel Roots.

Purpose: To see how the gospel is rooted in history and prophecy.

Group Discussion. These questions are designed to help the group to warm up to each other. No matter how well a group may know each other or how comfortable they may be with each other, there is always a stiffness that needs to be overcome before people will begin to talk openly. A good question will break the ice and get people thinking along the lines of the topic of the study These questions can reveal where our thoughts or feelings need to be transformed by Scripture. This is why it is especially important not to read the passage before the question is asked. The passage will tend to color the honest reactions people would otherwise give, because they are of course supposed to think the way the Bible does.

This question is designed to get the group thinking about how family histories give us a sense of identity and continuity with the past. The rest of the study will look at how Mark roots the gospel in Jewish history and prophecy.

Question 1. This question should be used to overview the whole passage, noting how verse 1 announces its themes. The idea here is to see that Mark is not a disinterested observer but a committed believer. Encourage the group to think about the significance of each key word or phrase: *beginning, gospel* (good news), *Jesus Christ, the Son of God*. What we learn here Jesus' contemporaries would only have learned gradually through their interaction with him.

Question 2. The quotations Mark cites are from Malachi 3:1 and Isaiah 40:3. Some people in your group may be disturbed that both quotations seem to be attributed to Isaiah. Explain, if necessary, that Mark may have attributed both to Isaiah because they both appeared on the same scroll or that he may simply have named the more significant prophet in drawing the two texts together. It was common rabbinic practice in Jesus' day to demonstrate one's knowledge of the Scriptures by drawing together separate but related texts. Notice how Jesus himself does this with Deuteronomy 6:4–5 and Leviticus 19:18 in Mark 12:30–31.

Question 4. Kings about to go on a journey often sent out a messenger to have the way prepared for them. Roads would be straightened, potholes filled in, bumps taken out. Mark draws on this kind of imagery from Isaiah's description of the Lord's coming to reign as king over his people. Numerous Old Testament passages describe God as king and foretell a day when he will reign unopposed over his people and creation.

Question 8. Craig S. Keener notes, "Disciples often served their teachers in the same ways that slaves would serve their masters, except for the most menial chores like taking off their masters' sandals" (*The IVP Bible Background Commentary: New Testament*, InterVarsity Press, 1993, p. 136).

Question 9. Though Jesus is without sin, he nevertheless identifies with sinners in coming to John for baptism. Donald English writes, "In baptism he shares the circumstances in which people become aware of their needs, precisely in order to meet those needs. He was to do that again and again in his ministry and supremely in his death and resurrection" (*The Message of Mark*, The Bible Speaks Today, IVP, 1992, p. 59).

Study 2. Mark 1:14–39. Portraits of Jesus.

Purpose: To begin to see Jesus as the servant–king who exercises his authority for the benefit of his subjects.

Question 1. Don't spend much time on this question. The goal is to mention a few initial impressions.

Question 2. Some people may have trouble answering this question. If so, get them to see the two assertions Jesus makes. Why is it good news that "the time has come" and "the kingdom of God is near"? How does Jesus ask people to respond to this good news?

Question 3. Be sure the group sees that the response of these four men shows the success of John the Baptist's ministry of preparation. This is the first of several questions throughout this guide designed to tie together material learned from previous studies.

Question 5. Some people may question the reality of demons—aren't they just primitive ways of describing mental and physical ailments? This would be plausible if the Gospels were not so careful about distinguishing physical ills from demon possession. Note that Simon's mother–in–law is not said to have a demon in the next incident. At least two factors might account for Jesus' silencing of the demon: (1) a desire to keep his identity hidden for the time being or (2) a desire not to have his identity revealed by an unreliable source (would you trust a demon to tell the truth?).

Question 8. Jesus' authority in carrying out his mission is strongly emphasized by such phrases as "at once" and "without delay." Notice all the areas of life to which Jesus' authority extends: teaching, demons, disease and people. If the group has difficulty answering the question, ask, "In what ways has the kingdom of God come near the people in these events?" The key issue here is to see that the kingdom is near because the king is present in the person of Jesus.

Study 3. Mark 1:40–2:17. Friend of Outcasts.

Purpose: To see that it is sinners who are invited to enter the kingdom.

Group Discussion. Depending on the group and their experience, this role play may go in different directions. Be prepared to discuss either a positive or negative response.

Question 1. Don't spend much time on this, but do allow the group to share their initial impressions concerning the resistance to Jesus.

Questions 2–3. Be sure that in answering these two questions the group notices that the way the man feels about himself affects his request. Even though he seems confident of Jesus' ability to heal, he questions Jesus' willingness to help him.

Question 4. Among other things, according to the Law, Jesus would become ceremonially unclean. He also risked getting the disease.

Question 5. Notice that Jesus' stern charges were oriented toward the man's good and not simply his own convenience. By fulfilling the requirements of the law (Lev 14:2–32), the man could be restored to his proper place in the social and religious fabric of society.

Question 7. We should not overlook the fact that the teachers of the law were quite right—if Jesus was not God, he was blaspheming by claiming for himself God's prerogative to forgive sins. By healing the paralytic, Jesus gave visible evidence that his words were true and that his authority was truly divine in nature.

Question 9. While the NIV puts the word *sinners* in quotation marks, other versions do not. The point here is that the Pharisees classified as a sinner anyone who failed to meet their rigid standards. They also failed to recognize that even the strictest Pharisee might be a sinner in God's eyes.

Question 10. Be sure the group notes both the physical and spiritual aspects of Jesus' work.

Question 11. Be sure to explore the social and psychological dimensions as well as the spiritual.

Question 12. If the group has trouble answering, ask, "What would the Pharisees have to admit about themselves before they would be ready to follow Jesus?"

Study 4. Mark 2:18–3:35. Conflict in Galilee.

Purpose: To see the causes of the growing opposition to Jesus and how viewing ourselves as members of God's family can reorient our attitudes toward obedience.

Question 2. The group may have difficulty understanding Jesus' two short parables. Encourage them to wrestle with what he says. Why, for instance, would it be inappropriate to fast at a wedding reception? What is Jesus suggesting about himself by talking about new cloth and new wineskins?

Question 3. Some members of the group may be troubled to learn that according to 1 Samuel 21 Ahimelech was the high priest when David ate the consecrated bread. Abiathar was Ahimelech's son who later became high priest (1 Sam 22:20). It was surely during his days that the event took place, just as we might say that during President Reagan's days the first atom bomb was exploded and the first trip to the moon was made—that is, the events took place during his lifetime if not during his administration. There is no need to raise this issue with the group unless one of the members brings it up.

Question 4. People may have difficulty seeing how Jesus' words rebuke a lax attitude toward the Sabbath. If so, ask, "If someone gives you a gift, is it right to despise it?" The point is that too lax a view of the Sabbath fails to see that God has made the Sabbath for our good. If we neglect it, we will miss the good he intends it to bring us.

Question 5. Be sure the group sees how the Pharisees' rigidity in keeping the law actually leads them to abuse it far worse than even they think Jesus does. Their rigidity leads to hate and murder.

Question 6. Non–Christians are not the only ones who object to our beliefs and practices. Sometimes our most vigorous opposition comes from those who are religious, who resemble the Pharisees of Jesus' day. Be sure to consider objections both groups might have. Jesus tried to help the Pharisees look at the intent of the law. They interpreted the law so rigidly that people got trampled underfoot. Jesus looked behind laws to see how they were intended for our benefit. Jesus was people–centered. The Pharisees were law-centered. This distinction can guide our behavior as Christians as well as our responses to those who object to our behavior.

Question 9. Everyone seems to know about someone who is convinced that they have blasphemed the Holy Spirit and are forever condemned. Two points are worth noting: (1) Jesus seems always ready to forgive any sin we are ready to confess; (2) the people here who are warned about blaspheming the Holy Spirit are about the last people who are concerned that this might be their problem. As Donald English puts it, "The sin against the Holy Spirit is portrayed as resolute attribution of God's gracious work to satanic origins. There is no forgiveness here because such an attitude is incapable of seeking it." (*The Message of Mark*, p. 89).

Question 12. Earlier in this passage we saw that the Pharisees had a rigid attitude toward God's commandments and other people. They evidently viewed themselves merely as God's slaves or subjects. This question helps us to explore how viewing ourselves as part of God's family can keep us from the error of the Pharisees.

Study 5. Mark 4:1–34. Kingdom Parables.

General note. The heart of this passage is contained in 4:1–24. Questions for 4:25–34 are found in the "Now or Later" section.

Purpose: To gain insight into the nature of God's kingdom and how we can become better, more creative evangelists.

Question 1. Be sure the group notices how many times the words *listen, hear* or *hearing* occur.

Question 2. Jesus doesn't consistently describe hearers as either soil or plants. Don't get bogged down in this. Just look at what happens to each combination.

Question 3. The parables clearly had the potential to conceal truth as well as to reveal it, and Jesus likely used parables to accomplish both ends. But it is not consistent with Jesus' character that his ultimate goal was to conceal the truth. The Isaiah passage Jesus quotes (Is 6:9–10) highlights Isaiah's responsibility to keep on proclaiming the truth despite the people's refusal to hear it. In a broader context we can see at least two ways that parables served Jesus' purposes. First, they weeded out people who were really not interested (more on this in question 4). Second, they had the potential to break through resistance to the truth, as Nathan's parable succeeded in breaking through David's defenses about his adultery with Bathsheba (2 Sam 12:1–14). Had Nathan confronted David directly, he might well have lost his head. By telling the parable Nathan succeeded in getting David to condemn his own actions. Encourage the group to keep watching how Jesus uses parables throughout the Gospel.

Questions 4–6. In light of the problem raised in question 3, these questions are designed to explore how people get to be on the inside or the outside (see also 3:34). Regardless of how we understand the role of God's sovereignty in this process, it is clear that individuals have a responsibility to act on what they are hearing. Also note that the parables are explained not just to the Twelve but to "others around him"—others, that is, who were inquisitive enough to remain with him and ask questions.

Question 7. In saying "to you has been given the secret of the kingdom," Jesus may mean no more than that he is about to explain the parable to those around him. Three factors, however, suggest that the secret of the kingdom is embedded within the parable of the sower: (1) Jesus' indication that this parable somehow unlocks all the rest (v. 13), (2) the fact that Jesus' remarks about the secret are sandwiched between the parable and its explanation, and (3) the amount of attention given to the parable and its explanation. Two strong possibilities arise from this understanding. First, the secret of the kingdom may be that Jesus is the farmer, the one who brings the kingdom by sowing the word. Second, the secret of the kingdom may be hearing the word and responding to it appropriately, that is, hearing the word, accepting it and acting on it, just as those who are asking for an explanation are doing. If the group is unable to reach a consensus, encourage them to keep thinking this over throughout their study of Mark.

Question 10. Be sure the group wrestles with the fact that the farmer does not know on what kind of soil he has scattered the seed until after he has scattered it. So he scatters the seed lavishly everywhere. Often in our evangelism we will discover that the seed we sow grows in some surprising soil. We are not called to judge the soil before we sow. What we once thought to be a hardened path may show itself in a new situation to be good soil.

Study 6. Mark 4:35–6:6. Fear & Faith.

Purpose: To explore how different kinds of fear and faith interact, and to learn how we can better turn our fears into faith.

General note. This passage is long, but if you keep the group moving and focusing on the big picture, you can cover it in the time allotted.

Questions 2–3. Some group members may be disturbed by what happened to the pigs and will bring it up early on in the study. If so, don't hesitate to go to questions 4–5 first and then come back to these.

Question 6. The purpose of this question is to get people thinking about why Jesus sometimes works to conceal his identity and at other times encourages that it be broadcast. A definite answer requires looking at the whole Gospel, so people should only explore a tentative solution at this point. Geography and whom he's speaking to are probably relevant factors. Here Jesus is speaking to a Gentile in a Gentile area. In previous instances he has silenced either demons or people in Jewish areas. (This question ties into the issue that scholars refer to as the Messianic secret in Mark).

Question 8. A little thought should convince the group that the questions people are asking and the offense they are taking are an outgrowth of fear.

Question 9. This question is designed to get group members to see that fear, like other human emotions, is not something we can turn on and off like a water spigot. What matters is what we do in the face of fear. Do we back away from God in our fear, or do we turn toward him? So the same fear may be good or bad depending on how we respond to it.

Now or Later. The questions here are designed to help the group to keep tying the Gospel together. Their study will be richer, and they will be much better prepared for the summary study if they keep trying to see the Gospel as a whole as they go along rather than as a series of isolated units. Be sure the group notices the threat of death in each incident here.

Study 7. Mark 6:6–52. Understanding the Loaves.

Purpose: To see how a proper vision of Jesus can keep our hearts soft and counteract the effects of overactivity.

Question 1. If necessary, break this question down. If the disciples take no provisions for themselves, who must they rely on? What were they to preach? What were they to do if they met resistance? Shaking the dust off their feet in leaving would have been a strong symbolic gesture of rejection—"Keep your own dust!"

Question 3. Herod shows symptoms of seed sown both among thorns and in rocky soil. What does this breakdown of categories suggest about the kinds of responses we may get as we share the good news of the kingdom?

Question 4. This is a tough question, but a significant one. The word *repent* (or *repentance*) occurs only three times in Mark's Gospel, yet each time it defines or summarizes a key aspect of the ministry of the person described. In 1:4 we see John the forerunner "preaching a baptism of repentance." In 1:15 we learn that Jesus' ministry was characterized by calling people to repent. Now we learn that those Jesus called to follow him went out and "preached that people should repent." Perhaps readers are wondering what happens to people who go out calling others to repent. *What happened to John?* (Here's the answer.) *What eventually happened to Jesus?* (Believers will already know.) *What then can his followers expect?*

Question 7. Herod, like the Pharisees, fails to be the kind of shepherd God desires for his people. Much of Mark's description of Jesus' feeding of the 5,000 uses language similar to that of Ezekiel 34:1–16. Thus we see Jesus fulfilling God's promise to come and be a shepherd to his people. We see this more clearly as readers of the Gospel than Jesus' contemporaries did, but this was one of the ways Jesus was revealing his true identity.

Question 9. The group may have trouble answering this question. If so, ask, "What should the feeding of the 5,000 from five loaves have revealed about Jesus?" Had the disciples understood Jesus' true identity, how might their reaction to his walking on the water have been different? This passage is full of allusions from the Old Testament like that of Ezekiel 34 mentioned in question

7. Jesus again and again does what only God did there—stilling the storm (Ps 107:23–32), feeding the crowd in the wilderness (Ex 16) and walking on water (Job 9:8–11). Those with eyes to see should be starting to understand who Jesus really is.

Question 10. Among the contributing factors might have been simple tiredness and hunger combined with ongoing demands (6:30–31). They also show a lack of vision and trust (6:36–37). Then there is further work to exhaustion in rowing against the wind in the middle of the night (6:48). Don't overlook that even their early success (6:12–13) may be another factor. They, like us, could become tired and hardened even while doing good.

Study 8. Mark 6:53–7:37. Violating Tradition.

Purpose: To see how tradition can harden our hearts to God's truth and how Jesus' assessment of human need cuts across the distinction between Jew and Gentile.

Question 1. Jesus goes about healing and making others clean by his contact with them. The Pharisees see themselves becoming unclean through their contact with others. What happens in our contact with the world? Are we changing it, or is it changing us?

Question 2. Isaiah 29:13 is referred to here. Isaiah "roundly denounced the religious leaders of his day,... and Jesus uses a quotation from this prophet to describe the tradition of the elders as 'rules taught by men'" (v. 7) (*NIV Study Bible*, Zondervan, 1995, p. 1504).

Question 3. It is, of course, always easier to point the finger at someone else's tradition rather than our own. ("Those fuddy-duddies insist on organ music and old hymns, which only turn off seekers. How can that honor God?" "This younger generation brings a band into church and mimics MTV. How can that honor God?") Try to get group members to identify traditions they actually are comfortable with that may not always honor God. Help them to see that their attitude toward the tradition and toward those who don't find it helpful may be what determines whether and how it honors God.

Question 6. You may want to explain that many of the traditions of the elders were embellishments on the Old Testament ceremonial law. Thus the observance of the law and the traditions served to distinguish Jews from Gentiles.

If, after some time for thought, the group is still struggling with this question, ask, "What aspect of our relationship with God do the ceremonial law and traditions emphasize—the external or the internal? What aspect does Jesus' standard emphasize? Jews and Gentiles obviously differ on the external issues, but do they differ on the internal issues?"

Questions 7–8. If the group has trouble with question 7, make sure they identify who the children are (the Jews), who the dogs are (the Gentiles) and what the bread is (his teaching and healing presence). Then the parable should be clear.

Many people are offended by Jesus' reference to Gentiles as dogs, a term that could be seen as highly offensive if we think of the wild scavengers typical of the day. But Jesus uses the diminutive "little dogs" that indicates pets kept in some household of the day, and William L. Lane argues what we are to see is a domestic scene—"The table is set and the family has gathered. It is inappropriate to interrupt the meal and allow the household dogs to carry off the children's bread" (*Commentary on the Gospel of Mark*, Eerdmans, 1974, p. 262). Thus Jesus' comment is not meant as an ethnic slur. On the other hand, Jesus may use the sentiment of his countrymen, who did on occasion refer to Gentiles as dogs, to overturn their racism. Don't allow the group to miss the fact that this woman is the only person who ever replies to one of Jesus' parables with a parable.

Study 9. Mark 8:1–9:1. Who Do You Say I Am?

Purpose: To have each member of the group confront personally the issue of who Jesus is and what difference he should make in our lives.

Question 3. Notice first the words and phrases that stress their need: *they had nothing to eat, three days, they will collapse, come a long distance, remote place* and so on. Then notice the words that stress the adequacy of the provision: *ate and were satisfied, seven basketfuls ... left over, four thousand men were present.*

Question 4. What evidence have the Pharisees shown that they would recognize a sign if one were given?

Question 5. If the group has trouble answering this, ask what Jesus condemned the Pharisees for in Mark 7 and what Herod's basic problem was in Mark 6.

Question 7. The purpose of this question is just to get the group to notice that the healing occurred in two stages. The significance of this observation is explored in question 11.

Question 8. The group may wonder why people would say that Jesus was Elijah. As we saw in study one, Malachi had prophesied that Elijah would come before the day of the Lord (Mal 4:5). As a result, the Jews of Jesus' day expected a prophet like Elijah to come before the Messiah.

Question 9. Peter's view of the Christ (or the Messiah) was likely that of his fellow Jews who expected a political leader, someone who would liberate them from Roman rule and restore their national pride. Such a view left no room for suffering and death.

Question 11. We are so used to seeing Peter's confession as a clear realization of who Jesus is that we often fail to see that only gradually did he learn what it meant. Peter's understanding needed a second touch as well.

Now or Later. If the group takes a whole session for review, it is important that each member prepare individually for the discussion.

Review of Mark 1–8.

Purpose: To summarize and explore the implications of what the group has discovered about the gospel and the kingdom thus far.

Question 1. Be sure the group catches the kingdom focus of the gospel as Jesus proclaimed it.

Question 4. If the group seems stumped, you might press further as follows: How would seeing Jesus as king and calling people to allegiance to him and his kingdom counteract an accept-Jesus-into-your-heart-and-do-as-you-please attitude?

Question 7. If the group has trouble answering, you could explain that most Jews were looking for a political Messiah, someone to lead them in overthrowing the Romans. What might have happened if Jesus had gone about announcing himself as the Messiah or Christ? Then, too, apart from a history of his deeds, what would have happened had he gone about announcing he was God?

For advanced groups you may wish to delve deeper into Jesus' use of the phrase "Son of Man." Jesus has used the phrase "the Son of Man" four times so far (2:10, 28; 8:31, 38). With hindsight it is rather easy to see that Jesus was speaking about himself and alluding to his role as Messiah. Jesus' hearers, however, would not likely have heard him that way. To them the phrase "Son of Man" would likely have sounded like another way of saying *man* (as in Psalm 8:4, where it means just that). Thus 2:28 might have sounded like this: "The Sabbath was made for man, not man for the Sabbath. So man is Lord even of the Sabbath." Only gradually would it have dawned on people that Jesus was talking about himself. Why might Jesus have spoken of himself in this roundabout way? What specifics thus far has Jesus revealed about himself in this way? How might this tie in with the question of why Jesus tries to silence some people he heals and encourages others to tell what he has done?

Part 2: Why Did Jesus Come? Mark 9–16

Study 10. Mark 9:2–32. Suffering & Glory.

Purpose: To examine the relationship between suffering and glory, human weakness and divine power.

Question 1. Moses and Elijah are representative of the law and the prophets. What company then does this put Jesus in? The prophecies of Deuteronomy 18:14–22 and Malachi 4:5 reveal even further significance in their presence.

Question 2. At least five events present themselves as possible fulfillments of Jesus' prediction—the transfiguration, the resurrection, the ascension, the day of Pentecost and the second coming. The second coming is the only one of these not to occur within the time frame Jesus mentions. All the rest anticipate the full glory of the second coming, giving glimpses of the power that will be fully revealed then. The review of Mark 9–16 in the "Now or Later" section of study twenty will ask the group to consider yet another possible fulfilment of this prophecy.

Question 3. Be sure the group sees that listening involves obedience. When your mother used to ask you, "Did you hear me?" she wasn't asking a question about your hearing ability but about your obedience.

If time allows, you might preface this question by saying: In this account God's voice is heard for a second time in Mark's Gospel, the first being in 1:11. What purposes are accomplished by God's affirmation here?

Question 4. If the group has difficulty answering this question, remind them of how we saw in study one that John the Baptist was fulfilling the role of Elijah as predicted in Malachi. Then look at what happened to John in Mark 6:14–29. Lane comments, "It is necessary to assume that the phrase 'even as it is written of him' has reference to the prophet Elijah in the framework of his historical ministry [for example, see 1 Kings 19:2, 10]. No passage of Scripture associates suffering with Elijah's eschatological ministry" (*Commentary on the Gospel of Mark*, p. 326, note 35).

Question 6. William Lane comments on Jesus' words "O unbelieving generation": "Jesus' poignant cry of exasperation is an expression of weariness which is close to heart–break.... This is brought into sharp relief when his exclamation is seen to be a personal word addressed to the disciples, who alone had failed at the crucial moment. Although they had been privileged to be with Jesus and possessed the charism of healing, they had been defeated through unbelief when they stood in his place and sought to exercise his power" (*Commentary on the Gospel of Mark*, p. 332).

Question 11. Note especially that the young boy appeared to suffer to the point of death before he was restored.

Study 11. Mark 9:33–50. The First & the Last.

Purpose: To explore the ways self–judgment and a servant attitude can promote Christian unity.

Question 2. If the group seems to struggle with this question, ask them what segments of society Jesus' followers came from and what segments of society his opponents came from. Be sure the group sees Jesus as the supreme example of the servant destined to be the greatest of all.

Question 8. The group may have trouble answering this question. If so, you might ask, "Would cutting off a hand or foot really keep us from sinning? If not, what would?" Sometimes we "spiritualize" Jesus' words to make them easier on ourselves, but spiritualizing here doesn't soften Jesus' words. The point is that it would be well worth plucking out an eye or cutting off a foot if that would keep us from sinning. But the effect would only be to produce blind and lame sinners. The root of our problem lies deeper, and we must confront it there.

Question 9. Fire in the earlier verses is clearly linked with judgment or testing. Salt is a common image for purification. How then are Christians purified by judgment or testing?

Question 10. If the group has trouble answering the first part of the question, move them on to the second part by asking, "Jesus seems to link having salt in yourselves with being at peace with one another. Does that shed any light on what having salt in yourself might mean?" The group should see that judging ourselves rather than one another contributes to peace and unity.

Question 12. Jesus offers several limitations in verses 40–50. We would, for instance, rightly oppose those who are genuinely against us or those who would cause little ones who believe in him to sin. William Lane argues that "little ones" here refers not to children but to fellow believers (*Commentary on the Gospel of Mark*, pp. 345–46).

Study 12. Mark 10:1–31. New Relationships.

Purpose: To explore some of the moral and social implications of the gospel.

General note. This study has more questions than some others, but many of them don't take long to answer. Pace yourself and you can still finish the study easily in time.

Question 3. The group may have some strong feelings about this issue. Try to help them listen to one another and to support their conclusions from the passage. A possible alternative to the view that Jesus intended an absolute prohibition of divorce is that he meant only to assert God's ideal for marriage, an ideal that he recognized that fallen human beings would not always live up to. He thus spoke in exaggerated terms meant to discourage all divorce in principle but not to prohibit divorce in every circumstance. Although no exceptions are included in Mark's account, Matthew records a slightly different version of Jesus' words, which is not cast in absolute terms (Mt 19:9). The group may want to explore the significance of this difference, but be careful not to spend too much time on this issue.

Question 4. "According to rabbinic law a man could commit adultery against another married man by seducing his wife (Deut. 22:13–29) and a wife could commit adultery against her husband by infidelity, but a husband could not be said to commit adultery against his wife. This sharp intensifying of the concept of adultery had the effect of elevating the status of the wife to the same dignity as her husband and placed the husband under an obligation of fidelity" (Lane, *Commentary on the Gospel of Mark*, p. 357). Lane also notes that Jewish law did not recognize the right of a woman to divorce her husband, though Roman law did (p. 358).

Question 6. The man seeks a response in terms of activity meriting eternal life. Ultimately Jesus gives him an answer that is based on relationship—"Come, follow me." Yet that relationship is not devoid of social implications.

Question 7. Of course, Jesus' illustration points to the fact that it is not only hard but impossible for the rich to be saved on their own. God must work. This passage highlights a paradox of the gospel—that we contribute nothing to our salvation, but we must give all to be Jesus' disciples. The group may struggle with the implications of Jesus' command to the rich man to "go, sell everything you have and give to the poor." Two extremes probably should be avoided: (1) assuming this command is universal and applies to all would-be disciples and (2) assuming that the problem is purely one of attitude and that would-be disciples who love the Lord more than their wealth may keep it. Don't let the group get off easy on this issue.

Question 9. The Pharisees come to Jesus not with openness and receptivity but with guile and a desire to entrap him. The rich young man asks an honest question but is calculating and unwilling to give himself wholeheartedly in faith to Jesus. Which kinds of unchildlike behavior are you most tempted to engage in?

Study 13. Mark 10:32–52. Blindness & Sight.

Purpose: To emphasize the servant role in Christian discipleship.

Question 5. The Old Testament speaks frequently of the cup of God's wrath (see, for example, Ps 75:8 and Is 51:17–23). Lane notes that "in popular Greek usage the vocabulary of baptism was used to speak of being overwhelmed by disaster or danger" (*Commentary on the Gospel of Mark*, p. 380).

Question 6. This theme is also seen in 9:35 and 10:31.

Question 7. Encourage group members to think about the whole range of their relationships. Do they have a friend, a spouse, neighbor that they could be more of a servant to? Is there a need in their community or a project through their church that could use their help?

Question 8. Don't overlook what Bartimaeus is able to "see" about Jesus even though he is blind. The name Bartimaeus is Aramaic for "son of honor."

Question 11. The story of Bartimaeus, "son of honor," not only shows Jesus' compassion and authority to heal, it has strong symbolic force within Mark's narrative. Notice first Bartimaeus's form of address—"Son of David"—which carried strong messianic overtones. These messianic overtones are all the more significant when we see Jesus opening Bartimaeus's eyes (see Is 35:5) and his imminent entry into Jerusalem. Not only does Bartimaeus recognize Jesus' ability to heal, but he is also prepared to submit himself to Jesus' authority—the NIV's *Rabbi* is actually the heightened form *Rabboni* ("my master," "my lord"). Then given the choice to go—his own way, presumably—Bartimaeus chooses to follow Jesus "along the road." This, of course, is the road to Jerusalem and Jesus' suffering and death. The significance of his choice is all the greater when we realize that "the road" or "the Way"—the same Greek word is used here and in Acts 19:9—later becomes a common term for the Christian faith.

Study 14. Mark 11:1–25. Palm Sunday.

Purpose: To better understand righteous anger and how a spirit of forgiveness is necessary when praying for God's judgment.

Question 2. Jesus is fulfilling Zechariah's prophecy about the Messiah's entry into Jerusalem (Zech 9:9–10). Surprisingly, at least to most Jews of Jesus' day, he comes as a man of peace, riding on a donkey rather than a warhorse. Be sure the group notices what the people did as well as what they said.

Despite how clearly we can see that Jesus was entering Jerusalem as Messiah, the people looking on probably did not. They undoubtedly saw Jesus as an important person, but may have seen him only as an important teacher on a special mission to Jerusalem. Their shouts, though loaded with messianic significance, were excerpts from Psalm 118 and other songs sung regularly on the way to Jerusalem each spring and fall for the major festivals. For further details, see Lane's *Commentary on the Gospel of Mark*, pp. 393–94, 396–97.

Question 3. For the context of Jesus' comments from the Old Testament, see Isaiah 56:4–8 and Jeremiah 7:1–11.

Questions 5–6. Fig trees and vines are often used as symbols of Israel's faithfulness to God. God comes to his vineyard looking for grapes and figs, that is, righteousness and justice and mercy. Thus looking for fruit on the fig tree represents what Jesus is looking for in the temple. See, for example, Jeremiah 8:13 (RSV, the NIV obscures this verse); 29:17; Hosea 9:10–16; Joel 1:7; Micah 7:1–6.

The group is apt to struggle with why Jesus curses the fig tree when "it was not the season for figs." It is probably most helpful to see this as an acted parable of the judgment that the temple faces. For those being judged, judgment seldom comes when expected.

Question 9. As he spoke these words, the Mount of Olives would have been in view. Zechariah prophesied that the Lord will one day return to the Mount of Olives to judge his enemies and to establish his kingdom (14:1–11). As his feet touch the Mount, it will move out of the way. Note that this understanding of prayer to move mountains is consistent with the judgment theme found in the incidents in the temple and with the fig tree.

Study 15. Mark 11:27–12:27. Tempting Questions.

Purpose: To better understand the role of answering and asking questions in Christian discipleship.

Group Discussion. If all the members of your group are Christians, you could ask, "What are some of your favorite (or least favorite) trip–up questions from unbelievers about the faith? How have you answered such questions?"

Question 2. The chief priests, the teachers of the law and the elders are setting a trap for Jesus. If he answers "from heaven" or "from God," they will charge him with blasphemy If he answers "from men," then they will claim he has no right to do what he's doing.

Question 5. The parable of the tenants is rich in meaning, especially in light of its allusion to Isaiah's Song of the Vineyard (Isaiah 5:1–7).

Question 6. The Scripture Jesus cited was Psalm 118:22–23. It "refers to one of the building blocks gathered at the site of Solomon's Temple which was rejected in the construction of the Sanctuary but which proved to be the keystone to the porch" (Lane, *Commentary on the Gospel of Mark*, p. 420). Modern distinctions between cornerstones, keystones and capstones will likely confuse the issue here. NIV's "capstone" is probably the least satisfactory translation of the Greek since it often connotes a finishing stone without structural significance. Either a keystone or cornerstone—either of which is vitally linked to the structural soundness of a building or arch—is meant.

Question 8. The Roman denarius brought to Jesus likely bore the inscription "Tiberius Caesar Augustus, Son of the Divine Augustus." Lane explains that the first part of Jesus' response shows that Jesus believed that civil authority has a rightful place in society and that he opposed a theocratic state, that is, a nation run by religious authorities. The second part of Jesus' response, however, shows that he objected to the idolatrous claim on the coins that Caesar was God (see *Commentary on the Gospel of Mark*, p. 424).

Question 10. Jesus' answer to the Sadducees in verse 26 is not as weak as it might first sound to modern ears. The formula "the God of Abraham, the God of Isaac, and the God of Jacob" is a reminder of God's covenant faithfulness. Lane summarizes, "It is inconceivable that God would provide for the patriarchs some partial tokens of deliverance and leave the final word to death, of which all the misfortunes and sufferings of human existence are only a foretaste. If the death of the patriarchs is the last word of their history, there has been a breach of the promises of God guaranteed by the covenant, and of which the formula 'the God of Abraham, of Isaac, and of Jacob' is the symbol" (*Commentary on the Gospel of Mark*, p. 430).

Study 16. Mark 12:28–44. An End to Questions.

Purpose: To underscore the relationship between love for God and love for neighbor and to further explore who Jesus is.

Question 1. According to the *NIV Study Bible*, "Jewish rabbis counted 613 individual statutes in the law, and attempted to differentiate between 'heavy' (or 'great') and 'light' (or 'little') commands" (p. 1516).

Question 3. The teacher is drawing together insights from 1 Samuel 15:22; Proverbs 21:3 and Hosea 6:6. Contemporary burnt offerings and sacrifices include various religious duties and activities, such as singing in the choir, teaching Sunday School or serving on church committees. All these things are good and helpful in their own right. But if they stand in the way of our loving God and our neighbor rather than being the means for doing so, we need to reevaluate our involvement. What other activities can you think of that are current-day burnt offerings and sacrifices?

Question 6. In 11:27–33 Jesus silences his opponents with his own question and refuses to answer theirs. In 12:1–12 he tells a parable which holds up a mirror to those who oppose his activity and teaching. In 12:13–17 he sees through his opponents' hypocrisy and still manages to answer them, but outside the parameters they expected. In 12:18–27 he points his questioners to Scripture and shows them how they fail to understand it and the power of God. In 12:28–34 he finds a genuine questioner and commends him on his insight. How can we learn to see behind people's questions and answer them wisely?

Question 7. Jesus is quoting David's words from Psalm 110:1. Be sure the group understands clearly that only a Christ who is both fully human and fully divine can be both lord and descendant.

Question 8. It is not enough just to call Jesus "Lord." We need to learn to obey him. As Luke records it, Jesus asks each of us, "Why do you call me, 'Lord, Lord,' and do not do what I say?" (Lk 6:46). The Christian life is a daily journey in learning to conform our lives to Jesus' lordship.

Now or Later. We learned in study one that Mark saw the coming of John the Baptist and Jesus in light of Malachi 3:1. This question shows us again Mark's concern to see Jesus as a fulfiller of prophecy.

Study 17. Mark 13. Keep Watch.

Purpose: To better understand Jesus' predictions concerning the fall of Jerusalem and his return, and to explore what it means to be alert for his return.

Questions 1–2. Make sure the group notices that the disciples are asking about the destruction of the temple. Jesus' answer is broader than their question; he enlarges the discussion to include the end (the last things).

Question 3. In Acts 5:35–37 Gamaliel mentions two false messiahs—Theudas and Judas the Galilean. First–century Palestine saw a variety of messianic movements, two of which were involved in Jewish revolts against the Romans in A.D. 66–70 and again in A.D. 132–135. The first of these revolts led to the destruction of Jerusalem, which Jesus predicts here. Given that Jesus has promised one day to return himself, he forewarns his disciples not to be taken in by false claims. On these and other revolutionary movements, see W. J. Heard, "Revolutionary Movements," in *Dictionary of Jesus and the Gospels*, ed. Joel B. Green, Scot McKnight and I. Howard Marshall (InterVarsity Press, 1992), pp. 688–98.

Question 5. Because the issue here is complicated and many people have definite views, this question is designed to help the group appreciate the strength of different points of view. It isn't necessary to achieve consensus on this issue; questions 8–11 get at the crucial issue.

Even expert opinion is divided on these issues. Lane notes that Luke, without mentioning "the abomination that causes desolation," clearly points to the events of A.D. 70 with armies surrounding Jerusalem. Josephus attributes the destruction of the temple to abuses of the Zealots who held up there from fall to spring A.D. 67–68. He accuses them of all sorts of crimes and wandering about in the Holy of Holies, even committing murder there. He sees the culmination of these abuses ("the abomination that causes desolation") in vesting as high priest a low-class priest by the name of Phanni. It is possible that many early Christians would have sympathized with Josephus's sentiment. (See Lane's *Commentary on the Gospel of Mark*, p. 469, as well as the whole discussion on pp. 465–73.)

F. F. Bruce holds that Josephus caricatures the Zealots and that his testimony is not to be trusted. He sees fulfillment of the "abomination that causes desolation" in the Roman sacrifices offered at the temple court at its destruction. (See F. F. Bruce, *New Testament History*, MMS, 1969, pp. 257, 383.)

Lane and Bruce differ on the details while agreeing that "the abomination that causes desolation" has already appeared in the temple during the events culminating in the destruction of the temple in A.D. 70. A further fulfillment, still to come, may parallel the events described in 2 Thessalonians 2:3–4 when the "man of lawlessness ... sets himself up in God's temple, proclaiming himself to be God" or when he performs some act of desecration (see Robert L. Thomas, "1, 2 Thessalonians," in *The Expositor's Bible Commentary*, ed. Frank E. Gaebelein, Zondervan, 1978, 11:322).

Question 7. This question is designed to bring out the cosmic character of the distress in verses 24–27 in contrast to the local character of those in verses 5–23. This is one piece of evidence that may suggest a difference in time between the destruction of Jerusalem and the return of Christ. One way to view the structure of Mark 13 is as follows: (1) 13:1–23—description of local signs associated with "these things," the destruction of the temple; (2) 13:24– 27—description of cosmic signs associated with "that day," the return of Christ; (3) 13:28–31—the surety that the temple will be destroyed within a generation; (4) 13:32–36—the uncertainty of when Christ will return.

Questions 9–11. Regardless of how we resolve the question of signs and of timing, Jesus above all urges us to be ready. Here is a point on which the group should clearly agree.

Study 18. Mark 14:1–42. The Betrayer Approaches.

Purpose: To empathize with Jesus in his last hours before the crucifixion and to explore a variety of discipleship issues: priorities, the Lord's Supper, the necessity of Jesus' death, and human failure.

Question 3. Be sure to explore the legitimacy of some of the objections, especially in light of Jesus' own teaching. See, for example, Mark 6:8–9 and 10:21.

Question 4. The issue is whether it is ever right to spend money on stained glass, pipe organs, padded pews and carpeting for our places of worship while some people in the world are going hungry. It is unlikely that the group will reach consensus in a short time. The question is intended to raise the issue and provoke thought. Don't spend too much time on this.

Question 6. Since the Reformation, the significance of Jesus' words "this is my body" and "this is my blood of the covenant" have divided not only Catholics from Protestants but also various Protestant traditions from one another. The Catholic view, known as *transubstantiation*, holds that the elements of bread and wine are transformed into the actual body and blood of Christ, and that only the *appearance* of the bread and wine remain. Among the Reformers, Zwingli took the most extreme position in the opposite direction, holding that the bread and wine are merely symbols and that the celebration of the Lord's Supper is a memorial of Jesus' death. Most Baptists today have followed Zwingli's lead. Luther's position is sometimes known as *consubstantiation*. He held that Christ's body and blood are present together with the bread and wine of the sacrament. Calvin and other Reformers, followed by most Presbyterians and Anglicans today, held that Christ is truly present in the sacrament but made available only to believers through faith.

Question 9. Notice that Jesus here again is an example of what he is asking of his disciples. The spirit in verse 38 may be the Holy Spirit. If so, Jesus' words here are a reminder to the disciples of the resources that are theirs as they confront their own weakness.

Study 19. Mark 14:43–72. Betrayed!

Purpose: To explore the variety of motives involved in Jesus' betrayal and abandonment, and to draw warnings and encouragement for times of our own testing as disciples.

Question 2. If people have questions about verse 47, John 8:10–11 tells us that it was Peter who struck the servant.

Question 3. In trying to save himself, the young man loses what little he has. Some have thought this young man was Mark himself, included anonymously in this account of Jesus' betrayal.

Question 5. In identifying himself as the Christ, Jesus goes on to link himself with "the Son of Man" described in Daniel 7:13–14. This is the first time his public use of the title "Son of Man" would have had clear messianic overtones.

Sometime on their own, advanced groups may wish to review Jesus' use of the term "Son of Man" throughout the whole Gospel. For the use of the term in Mark 1–8, see the note on question 7 of the review study of the "Now or Later" section of study nine. What further insights into the questions asked there are seen through the use of "Son of Man" in the last half of Mark (9:9, 12, 31; 10:33; 13:26; 14:21, 41)?

Question 6. The issue here is that if Jesus was not God, he was clearly guilty of blasphemy.

Study 20. Mark 15–16. Victory Snatched from Defeat.

Purpose: To better understand the significance of Jesus' death in order to strengthen our commitment to sharing the gospel with others.

Questions 2–4. Questions 2–3 may be answered by the group in responding to question 1. If so, you might want to reword question 4 as follows: "How can we keep from succumbing to Pilate's temptation of wanting to do right but not doing it?"

Question 6. If the group has difficulty seeing the relevance of 10:38 and 14:36, ask, "If Jesus had been drugged, how would it have blunted his full participation in the cup of suffering he voluntarily took on?"

Question 7. Note especially "he saved others ... but he can't save himself." Be sure the group sees that it is precisely *because* he did not save himself that he is able to save others. There are several other ironies in the passage. Take time to answer this key question fully.

In verse 34 Jesus quotes the first verse of Psalm 22. If the group has time, it can be very instructive to read the whole psalm looking for all it points to in Jesus' experience on the cross.

Question 8. While the centurion's confession may not have been a full–blown testimony of faith, he is not saying Jesus was merely "a son of God" as some translations suggest. No article is present in the Greek because the predicate noun comes first just as in John 1:1 ("the Word was God"). (See Lane's *Commentary on the Gospel of Mark*, p. 571 n. 69)

Question 12. Two issues come to the forefront here. First, why does the Gospel seem to come to such an inconclusive close? The group may be helped in thinking about why this might be appropriate by reconsidering how Mark opens his Gospel (1:1). The second issue concerns ending the Gospel on a note of fear. But, as we have seen, especially in study six, not all fear is bad. In fact, this last sentence of the Gospel could just as well, if not better, be translated, "They said nothing to anyone, because they were filled with awe." There are several instances in Mark's Gospel of people who respond with fear or awe to significant new revelations (see 4:41; 5:15, 33, 36; 6:50; 9:6, 32). Thus the Gospel ends on a note of awe and wonder at what God has done.

Now or Later. If you give this review a whole session, be sure to encourage your group to prepare in advance.

Review of Mark 9–16.

Purpose: To summarize and explore the implications of the last half of Mark's Gospel.

General note. Don't skip this review! At least not if you want to get the most out of your time in Mark. The rewards of looking back and drawing together certain themes are well worth the effort.

Question 5. If the group fails to consider the cross as a key display of Jesus' glory, you may want to ask at what points Jesus' identity as the Son of God is declared and recognized (see 1:1, 11; 9:7; 14:61–62 and 15:39).

Question 6. In answering this question, as in answering question 5, it is key to see that the centurion sees Jesus' glory (his identity) on the cross (15:39).

James Hoover (MDiv, Gordon Conwell) was IVP's long-time associate editorial director and senior editor for IVP Academic.